THE INSPIRED

Travel Solo with Confidence and Joy

Kim Dalzell

NutriQuest Press

The characters and events portrayed in this book are fictitious. Family members are the exception, and their names are used with their approval. Any similarity to real persons, living or dead, is coincidental and not intended by the author.

ISBN-13: 9780971255814

Cover design by: K. Dalzell

Printed in the United States of America

DISCLOSURE: If you choose to order nutrition products at https://kimdalzell.juiceplus.com/us/en-us I will earn a small commission. Thank you for supporting a girl's wanderlust.

CONTENTS

DEDICATION

It takes a strong person to travel solo and an even stronger person to encourage and support someone's wanderlust. I want to thank Mark, my mate in life, for his unwavering support of my inspired travels and more.

SHIFTING YOUR MINDSET

Have you ever felt the pull of something you wanted to do, only to be held back by fear? It is a shared experience, but are you aware that your fear can be a powerful driver to create a more inspired life?

I felt this unexpected pull while visiting a small Midwest town where I was waiting overnight to deliver a nutrition presentation the next day. After dinner, I had time to kill, so I walked to the local hardware store and eyed a Redbox near the propane tank exchange station. What a find! A movie kiosk in this four-stop-light town! The film that caught my eye had backpackers on the jacket cover. Being an avid hiker, it was an obvious choice. I returned to my room at the Circle S motel, propped myself up with pillows, tucked myself into the white, crisp bed sheets, and popped the disk into my laptop.

The feature highlighted a father's quest to honor his estranged son, who died while trekking on the Camino de Santiago. This famous pilgrimage attracts people worldwide interested in a spiritual, cultural, or fitness journey. Many commit to the whole thing—a grueling five hundred miles through southern France and northern Spain. Some people walk together, and some walk alone.

Watching the film, I felt a physical response that I couldn't ignore. My palms were clammy, and my heart raced. I even dreamed about hiking through the Pyrenees mountains in France that night. I took this as a sign. What about if I walked the entire Camino—alone? This idea was a turning point for me, a moment of awareness and empowerment that would change my life forever.

When offering life advice, I have often told my children to "find the juice." I explained to them that "the juice" is about experiencing pure joy around something that elevates you beyond the physical world. You know it when you feel it. And the juice of life is different for each one of us.

There was just one small problem with this Camino idea. I had never traveled alone for pleasure and, indeed, had not traveled overseas alone. I was petrified and overwhelmed just thinking about the many logistics I needed to figure out before I embarked upon this journey! I began rationalizing why I couldn't go: I had two teenagers, a thriving private practice, and a husband who traveled for a living. Oh, yeah, and what about the dogs? This could never work.

But the feeling of going grew more robust, and I kept dreaming about the possibility of it all. I mentioned the trip again to my husband during a morning hot tub soak. He squinted his eyes at me and said, "You should go. We'll figure things out here." I gulped dryly at the unexpected support and acknowledged that nothing stopped me except for me.

Don't you hate it when people take every excuse away from you? Now I had no choice! It was time to let it go or get going!

Over the next several months, to get comfortable with the idea, I tirelessly researched everything about the pilgrimage. I read books and looked at trail maps. I fumbled through transportation plans. I made and remade packing lists. I bought a large rubber sink plug. Someone told me that it would be necessary to handwash my underwear and socks. I was in way over my head. I mentally beat myself up. Why didn't I have more common sense about these things? But, slowly, over time and in a very imperfect way, I got ready to leave my familiar surroundings and answer the call of the unknown.

In the summer of 2013, I completed the entire Camino solo, carrying twenty-three pounds on my back for 31 days with only ten words of Spanish in my communication repertoire.

Looking back on that trip, I realized something important. It might seem to outsiders that I just boldly took off for an adventure, but I had been slowly building the confidence to travel solo without knowing it. My belief in myself did not happen overnight, and many seemingly unrelated choices contributed to my bravery, like when I decided to watch Sweet Home Alabama alone in a movie theatre because no one else was available to join me. I'm a solid Reese Witherspoon fan. That choice was a small step toward my independence but an essential one in the larger scheme.

After I completed the Camino, my world opened. I became a different person and closer to the real me. The buried teenage notion that I "would see the whole, wide world someday" resurfaced in my hungry, hopeful mind. I felt more confident. I realized that I could do hard things. And I was proud of myself for creating and tackling challenges I set for myself, not set by anyone else. It seems a little silly to say, but I became a celebrity to myself!

This book isn't about achieving a bold, adventurous solo travel goal. Whether you're considering joining a tour group as a solo traveler, meeting your long-distance friends in an exotic location, or navigating the subway system in an unfamiliar town, the confidence to travel solo is within your reach! I've written this book with someone like you in mind, sharing my emotional ups and downs and thought processes to encourage you to embrace a more self-assured version of yourself. You'll read about the perspective shifts and stress-free travel strategies I've mastered so you, too, can transform from someone who waits for others to someone who fearlessly explores the world as a solo nomad!

You know it's time to tick off some of those bucket list places. Get ready to get off the couch and get into the world!

The Juice

Santiago de Compostela, Spain

Blisters on blisters, heat, mud, rain, and cow manure. Pain in my knees, shoulders, and back. Strategically relieving myself roadside to not caring who sees. And most of all, finding a piece of me that I didn't realize was missing. Five hundred miles. At least that many smiles.

Thanks to the Way of St. James.

CALLING ALL SOLO SISTERS

About once a week, when I'm home, I attend a meet-up to expand my social circle and indulge my passion for talking about all things travel. If I'm lucky, I will meet someone who enjoys long-distance trekking or visiting foreign lands as much as I do. In that case, we'll hole up in the corner of the room and share entertaining and enriching stories of our respective past trips. While you can look online for where to get the best boat noodles in Bangkok, the wonderful thing about face-to-face interactions is that you have opportunities for real-time questions and explanations, which keep you engaged and excited about your travel dreams.

Be aware that in-person conversations usually prompt questions. When people find out I like to travel solo, they usually ask me why. My standard reply is that I have gypsy in my genes, which is true (I have German-Ukraine ancestry). This fact might explain some of my quirkiness and fondness for colorful scarves, but it isn't entirely forthright.

Women decide to go solo for many reasons, and I am no different. One solo sister shared with me, 'The reason I went on this trip was a strong conviction I felt inside that this was a good thing to do. I wanted it to be a turning point, like turning the page after a rough year. I wanted to have room to find out what it is like to only consider my thoughts, wants, and needs and to have time to contemplate and enjoy nature. I just really wanted to see if I would like my own company." Wherever you are in life, going solo can help you find meaning behind your life choices and circumstances. Solo travel may start as an escape, but it often brings your soul back home.

I've heard from heartbroken widows who are taking trips for the first time to honor their beloved spouses. Divorce or surviving a graduated marriage are two other life changes that may call for women to reclaim their independence by journeying into the world.

Others, like me, have a spouse with a different enthusiasm for travel or very different interests or hobbies. An injury or lack of interest in a particular sport sometimes keeps you from doing an activity together. You can avoid disappointment and resentment if you open the door to an honest conversation about what will serve you both when traveling.

Choosing to travel alone, as opposed to not having a travel partner, often invites judgment and negative responses. It helps to be prepared with a direct and confident explanation, as people are curious about why you want to travel alone. For example, a new friend recently asked me, "So, you travel... alone...and sometimes your husband travels alone...how does that work?" She could not imagine going on a holiday anywhere without her husband beside her. As you read this, you may be wondering about that too.

My answer: "I am fiercely independent. My husband is fiercely independent, too. Sometimes we travel together, but often we do not. He likes to scuba dive. I'm not much of a swimmer, so having diving weights around my waist, sinking me into the ocean's inky depths, doesn't appeal to me. I like hiking for multiple days, trudging through pelting rain if required to get across the mountains. My husband thinks that's a definition of unnecessary torture. So, it makes sense for us to go our separate ways sometimes. I won't apologize for being independent. Be happy for me. I get to do what I enjoy and offer the same to the person I love."

Open-mouthed for ten seconds, I expected her to give me a rousing "You go, girl!" Instead, she only sputtered, "Wow."

I took that as a sign of admiration. It might not have been. I don't care. And neither should you. Only some people will understand your wishes or need to travel solo. The first person that needs to understand is you. Send good thoughts to everyone and get on your way.

Now, when it comes to those closest to you, other elements may be at play. Your best-intentioned friends or caring relatives may call you crazy, careless, a poor mother, or a selfish partner for traveling solo. You may start second-guessing when they send you news about the latest tropical storm surging near your intended travel spot. And did you hear about the train strike in Europe?

Do you know where all of this is coming from? Fear. They fear for your safety (you do, too). They fear you will return to being a different person (you most likely will). They fear they will lose you (remind them why you value them in your life). Reassure them in every way possible, and then book that trip.

Now, if you are fortunate to have a partner who understands and supports your need for travel, that makes it easier to leave home. Be honest, after living with someone for years, don't you sometimes relish time away from them? You might be too polite to admit it to someone else, but at least admit it to yourself. If you need to feel better about things, play the kid card. Remind yourself that it is good to model independence and a spirit for adventure to your children. They can learn through your actions to stretch themselves.

The raw truth is that it took me a while to get there myself. At first, I was concerned that my relationship with my husband would suffer. I grew up with the idea that married people do everything together. Then, I realized I wouldn't bring my whole self to my relationship if I did not honor my needs. Over time, traveling solo helped me appreciate that I am an individual, not just one of two. I return with a renewed sense of joy around the routines of daily life and enjoy the comfort of being back home. And stories. I have exciting new stories to tell! I love me as a couple, and I love me.

Regardless of your reason for traveling solo, whether you are at a crossroads in your life because of an unforeseen or sad circumstance or are searching for more meaning and a deeper understanding of yourself, I encourage you to heed the call of your inner gypsy (genetic or symbolic). Solo travel can be a life-changing opportunity to create a new and improved version of a beautiful you.

One final note: If you think, "I could never go solo!" Think again. Soloing doesn't just involve hiking in the wilderness with peat up to your knees and eating leaves and insects. Okay, I am being a bit dramatic. I haven't eaten bugs except for termites, and that was on a trip where I strolled back from the rainforest to a cozy tree house in Belize and enjoyed wine with dinner that night. Like a midnight buffet on an Alaskan cruise, you can choose what feeds your spirit. You may consider going solo by taking a city tour, traveling away for the weekend with your best friend, or visiting a new museum. So, remember, there are many levels to going solo, as you will discover in the next chapter.

Above all, please don't ignore the call, solo sister, as it gets louder as time passes!

The Juice

Hiking the Reeks District, Bridia Valley, Ireland

Before I started, I had yet to learn what a stile was. By the time I finished, I had climbed about two hundred of them.

Novelty wears off no matter where you are or what you are doing.

And that's when you start to learn more about yourself. Once the thrill of "new" is over, how will you choose to embrace the same path forward?

Stiles have been placed along The Kerry Way so humans can cross over or through land boundaries while protecting livestock and avoiding boggy areas with deep pockets of water camouflaged by straw-colored grasses.

Stiles serve a good purpose and can mark the way. I kept telling my knees and hips that as I hoisted myself over the barriers, some six or seven steps high.

Day two began with a rocky, narrow saddle hike, crossing multiple streams. For most of the day, I was sandwiched between two mountain ranges, with nothing more to see than sharp rock faces dotted with violet wildflowers hanging onto their last few weeks of life.

I felt very alone, unprotected, and vulnerable.

With one long breath, I mustered my solo superpowers and pretended to be the female version of Bear Grylls's trekking in the wilderness. It helped me to ignore that I had packed lunch and wouldn't need to eat some stringy moss off a rock for my sustenance.

The thing about hiking through mountains is that you can't see over them to know where you are going. So, I dutifully followed the way markers and trusted I would eventually see civilization again.

I guess that's what this is all about. Trusting the signs along my journey and taking it one step at a time.

TRAVEL WITH A SIDE OF CONFIDENCE

It is entirely natural to have some anxiety about traveling alone. Think about it. Why wouldn't you expect to be nervous when encountering a new experience or the uncertainties of a foreign place?

Recently, I have become aware that I have accomplished many "solo" experiences in my everyday life. As a military spouse, wife of a pilot, and serial college student, I unwittingly groomed myself to stand on my own two feet and forge into the unknown! Each time I moved from my hometown to another state (and moved several times after that) or walked onto a university campus with students ten years younger than myself, I expanded my comfort zone. But it isn't just significant life changes that create growth. For example, I signed myself up for a wheel-throwing pottery class at the Colorado Springs Art Center (and I have lots of misshapen pots around the house to prove it). I didn't know a soul and had never thrown clay onto a spiraling table. I made out just fine, even if my pots didn't. My point is this: You are probably a more confident "soloist" than you think!

Take a minute now and review your life. What have you done alone? When did you face your fear, and did it anyway? Have you gone solo to a yoga class or sat alone in a new cafe to enjoy a slice of homemade carrot cake? Have you attended a friend's party without a mate? The skills needed to travel solo are just an extension of what you already know how to do. This realization changed my mindset and boosted my confidence to travel alone.

Get a pen and piece of paper out right now (or open your laptop or phone) and jot down some examples of when you have gone solo in your daily life. Everything counts! Once you start looking at your list, you will realize that you, too, have primed yourself your whole life to act like a solo sister!

Give yourself some grace, breathe deeply, and remember that each time you tackle a new obstacle, you are building more knowledge and confidence and are using your past experiences to help you along the way. This can be intimidating but exciting at the same time.

At the beginning of my solo travels, I would second-guess myself often. Was I catching the right train? Can I really trust Google Maps to get me back to my hotel? I continually asked strangers questions to reassure myself, and then, eventually, the need to ask others decreased, and I began internal problem-solving. I started to believe in myself and my skills. I've learned from my mistakes, and you will, too. Count on it.

Here's a mistake I will never forget: After missing an evening flight in Frankfurt, the airport information desk employee arranged a hotel transfer for me. I wasn't fussy; I only wanted to catch six hours of sleep before the following early morning flight. It took me over an hour to get to the recommended hotel, and I found no air conditioning or fan. Outside, below my open window, noisy tourists were fighting the sweltering summer temperatures by drinking down cold Pilsners until the wee hours of the morning. The restaurants nearby were closed, so my dinner became a chunk of cheese on white bread from a display case in the hotel lobby. I couldn't help but think the airport employee's family owned this place, and he got a kickback for sending another weary, naive traveler their way.

Exhausted, hungry, and overheated, clad in day-old underwear, I laid in bed spread eagle with ice-filled plastic cups under my armpits to cool off. There would be no sleep for me that night! After checking out the following morning, I sat in the hotel lobby at a small wooden table, waiting for my complimentary breakfast. My delight turned to disbelief when the hotel clerk placed a small plate before me. You guessed it! The same chunk of cheese on white bread from the display case! I laughed, and I cried. It wasn't fun then, but I had a hilarious story to tell my girlfriends when I returned home. Because of that experience, I now ask more questions before saying yes to recommendations. Live, sweat, and learn!

My latest solo goal was to become more confident about public transportation in foreign countries. There was a time when I felt safe only taking an expensive taxi from the airport to my hotel. My trip to Greece solidified my belief in my abilities when I successfully navigated an island-to-island ferry strike and then produced a Plan B when I discovered a national holiday would shut down sections of the metro system in Athens. But here's what did it for me: Carly Ann, a red-haired, fresh-faced young marketing professional, had missed the same flight back to the USA as me. At the airport, I overheard Lufthansa reps give her some options that didn't make sense. She looked lost and frustrated. I discreetly pulled her aside, gave her some vital information, and helped her get the flight and hotel options she deserved. I acknowledged her appreciation with a big smile, feeling good that she trusted my advice and that I could help her have a better travel experience. This story is a call to action for any seasoned solo sister: always take time to help another woman traveling solo. Be her angel. Someone has been yours in the past, after all.

For those with more exposure to traveling alone, you may be ready to up your game. Replace taxis with buses or subways. Consider a self-guided tour instead of joining a group. Arrive a few days earlier at your destination and enjoy some solo time before you meet a friend there. Try designing your perfect solo itinerary with one new element of challenge and book it!

If you are still getting ready to take the plunge, a great place to start building courage for solo travel is right in your hometown. For many, the significant barrier to traveling alone is dining out or going to an attraction alone, but many aspects of solo travel require you to challenge yourself.

Try these solo sister challenges (remember, you do these alone) to expand your comfort zone and build your solo travel confidence:

- Lounge in a busy coffee shop for 30 minutes.
- Dine in at a quick-service restaurant.
- Treat yourself to a full-service restaurant.
- Attend a movie matinee.
- Attend a movie on a Friday or Saturday night.
- Go to an art or history museum.
- Walk around a nearby city's downtown area.
- Visit a nearby park or zoo.
- Attend a theater production or local event.
- Spend the night at a nice hotel.
- Sign up for a city tour.
- Kayak, bike, or hike by yourself (tell someone your plans).

The great news is that building confidence for solo travel is circular: You need the experience to travel solo, and each time you travel solo, you gain more experience!

You will feel more comfortable with each exposure. Be aware it will feel different, so you might not like it at all! Keep persevering! If you desire to travel solo confidently, you must continue practicing doing things alone to feel in control and composed. One day, like me, you may thoroughly enjoy dining alone, touring a city solo, or trekking through a mountain gorge with only animals to keep you company. And you will be smiling at how far you have come. Now that's The Juice I am talking about!

The Juice

Grand Cayman, Stingray City

I thought it was a fun plan.

Take a catamaran out and swim in the ocean with a swirling family of stingrays.

I must admit I was a little nervous because, well, those guys are pretty big, and they look odd. And something different is always a bit scary.

In the water, there was a moment when I had the chance to approach one of these creatures. I had to decide quickly if I would be someone who admired something from afar or if I would embrace the convergence of two worlds - land and sea creatures together. I chose the latter.

Portobello mushroom-like belly, dark sandpaper topcoat, and piercing eyes that mirrored the darkest depth of the ocean. What a gentle creature!

It was surreal and beyond beautiful, and for this new(ish) swimmer, I felt like I truly belonged in the sea.

When we fully immerse ourselves in an experience, we transform. We become less afraid of things we do not know. And in a world of strife, comparison, and hatred for those unlike us, embracing the unknown helps us realize we are part of one big family here on Earth.

WHAT'S YOUR SOLO STYLE?

We met at a neighborhood coffee shop, claimed our plush, comfy chairs, and settled in to dish about the best travel destinations for women. I've been a part of this group for a few months now and enjoyed hearing about the different travel styles. Some of us were nature lovers, preferring long-distance solo hikes, while others enjoyed party cruises or city-filled social scenes.

Pam mentioned how safe she felt on her most recent trip and said she was proud to have done it solo. She excitedly reported, "I went to two national parks with an adventure tour company, and it was just awesome." Sheila responded with a sideways glance, "Oh, well, that technically isn't going solo, is it?" Mary added, "You stayed in the US, which isn't like going to a foreign country. So not too challenging, I'd say!"

In disbelief, I almost choked on my chai latte. These two women offered some strong opinions regarding what counts as going solo. If you talk to enough people, you'll learn that some believe you can only call yourself a solo traveler if you plan the entire trip and travel by yourself. Some consider you a solo traveler if you show up as a single, even if you join a group.

Whether you plan out every detail of your itinerary, share a room with a stranger, or take advantage of ready-made tours, you are a solo traveler when you travel by yourself for some or all of a journey. So, ignore the judgments and get ready to claim your unique solo style! The benefit of doing so is that you can become more aware of the trips you will enjoy the most without getting too far outside your comfort zone.

If you need more clarification about your solo style, keep reading!

The Connector

You are a natural people person.

You love to meet like-minded people.

You make new friendships quickly.

You enjoy group activities where you can be creative and interactive.

When you travel, you have a richer experience when you share special moments or events with others.

As a Connector, you typically enjoy soloing while joining a group (when you have not convinced your friends to join you). You will be happiest choosing full-day trip options with larger groups, taking night tours, and enjoying pub crawls or local food tours. Get creative with cooking or craft-making classes. You may enjoy staying in hostels or pensions, as many offer community spaces to encourage togetherness and sharing. Go where the people are gathered and connect away!

The Worldly Woman

You often think about how you can make the world a better place.

You enjoy supporting a culture or community.

You quickly lend a hand to foreign conservation projects.

You believe that travel can change an individual's perspective about the world.

You enjoy a chance to immerse yourself in other cultures.

As a Worldly Woman, you will likely enjoy attending culturally unique sporting events, volunteering for animal welfare projects, and visiting museums or historical sites to enrich your travel experience. Your trips will be fulfilling if you have time for fieldwork and exposure to community activities. Your choice of overnight accommodation might be rustic or refined. You might appreciate a homestay, where you can experience daily life from a local. Ecolodges may appeal to you as well. Guided or unguided, you will likely enjoy solo travel experiences connected to serving others and feeding your cultural awareness.

The Soul-O Sister

You crave opportunities to stretch your mind and comfort zone.

You thrive on experiencing new environments and cultures.

You use travel to nurture your body, mind, and spirit.

You believe that travel helps to expand horizons.

You have a natural tendency to be flexible in a group.

As a Soul-O Sister, you may enjoy visiting foreign countries with vastly different cultures. When you solo travel, consider taking a walking tour with a local guide, submerging yourself in a yoga retreat, self-guided hike, or small group wildlife trekking tour. You may wish to look for homestays, hostels, high-end hotels, or anything in between, depending on where you are and how social or secluded you want to be. You will likely enjoy solo journeying with dedicated quiet reflection and contemplation but can also appreciate time with like-minded people.

The Freedom Seeker

You follow your own path and create it as you go.

Your priority is to set new life goals and enrich your life.

Travel feels best when you feel free and untethered.

Nature and a sense of adventure reinvigorate you.

You have an internal drive to seek to understand yourself.

As a Freedom Seeker, you will likely enjoy solo journeying with an itinerary you developed yourself. You are more likely to enjoy camping or trekking experiences or unguided tours, where you can choose from various options that suit your mood for the day. You may prefer safari or wilderness tents, unique glass hotels in nature, or private ensuite rooms in quaint homes. You are open to landing in a new city and seeing what happens next. Overseas adventures and exclusive destinations are likely to be on your bucket list!

Remember that there is no single ideal solo style, and more than likely, you will evolve your style (if you wish) as you become a more seasoned traveler. Most solo travelers enjoy a mixture of frequently visited sights with once-in-a-lifetime experiences. You will become keenly aware of what type of trip makes you the happiest. For example, you might sign up to enjoy the social interaction of a group tour and then realize you want more downtime. That knowledge can help you make decisions about future trips.

I've gone through my own evolution over the years. When I first began traveling overseas, I loved visiting the cities of new countries. There is nothing quite like having a coffee outside a small cafe in Paris, admiring the artists who paint along the Thames in London, or navigating Bruges's quaint cobbled stone streets. Once I began hiking, trekking through national parks and reserves was more my style. Lately, though, I've been tacking on city tours at the end of my hiking time to deepen my understanding of the people and their culture.

The only way you will know your true solo style is to continue trying out every type of scenario and see what fits best!

The Juice

Stolen Moments at Serrano Glacier, Patagonia

I waited for this moment.

The crew secured the kayaks, the tents were up, and the group gathered around the mess tent to enjoy Chilean appetizers and celebratory pisco sours chilled with glacier ice.

I had a different idea.

Eschewing the planked walk to the observation deck, I chose instead to hike up a faint path that dissolved into the tall trees. To my delight, I came upon a steep drop-off much closer to the edges of the glacier lagoon.

My eyes followed the boulders along the coastline as my brain calculated: Scramble down those rocks, hands, and knees needed for that section over there, and I might get my feet wet if I can't hop over that piece. Yeah. Let's see how far I can go!

Although the coastline became impassable after a point, I reveled in the stolen moments I worked so hard for. Just me and the breathtakingly beautiful aquamarine shards of ice that made up the majestic Serrano Glacier.

LOSING CONTROL (IN A GOOD WAY)

Having been a solo wander woman for a while, I impulsively signed up for a group hiking tour of the Greek Isles with people I knew through a local meet-up. The group's itinerary was something I could have easily navigated on my own, hiking through gorges and along the coasts overlooking the Mediterranean Sea.

My goal in joining the group was to let someone else take control of the trip. Talk about being outside of my comfort zone! However, the group's leader was not only the founder of the meet-up and was well-liked; he was also a travel agent. It was time to sit back and enjoy the ride! I called this trip my un-solo experiment. And I failed miserably.

Some of you might be happy for others to plan out an entire trip for you. You can't imagine having to navigate all the little details of a holiday by yourself. That's what you pay a tour operator for! But if you are more like me, you want to take control. It takes work to hand over the reins to someone else. Think about the first time your teenage driver got behind the wheel of your new car. Do you get the picture now?

As the trek details became available, I immediately went into planning mode. I asked if I could change a few things to suit my needs. Luckily, the tour leader was very accommodating since I spoke up early enough to make some of these adjustments possible. I knew there would be many moments during the tour where I would not be in control and would need to follow someone else's agenda. Could I do it?

By day two, I had my answer. I had a tough time letting go of the need to know about all the details (Will I need to pack a lunch? Do I need to buy a ticket for entry into the gorge? How will we get back to the hotel after the hike?). I was frustrated by the lack of preplanning and communication. The truth is it all had to do with timing. I wanted the information sooner, not later. Many in the group were more easygoing and received the information as it was presented, so this was simply a case of someone doing things differently than I would have done.

I came to an embarrassing conclusion: I think I should attend a 12-step recovery meeting for Type A travel soloists, but I'm afraid I would want to take over the entire agenda and arrange a midnight hike somewhere.

Relinquishing control in a group environment is not the easiest thing to do, especially when you are used to traveling alone. And it's not just me. One of the most significant reasons women enjoy traveling solo is that they can make their own decisions without being influenced by others.

This was certainly the case for a solo sister I know. She told me she often deferred to her husband when choosing vacation activities for their family. They usually went to the beach and enjoyed water sports, but she preferred visiting the city for museums and the opera. She got tired of waiting for her spouse to say yes to her desired activities, so she recently has made it a point to attend theatre or musical productions everywhere she travels. She goes alone, and she is much happier.

There are some practical reasons for solo travel, too. For example, if you are health conscious and others are not, you must decide if you can keep your daily habits intact and still participate with the group.

Sometimes, you can't keep up with others if you have limited mobility. You may be unable to kayak or zipline and feel isolated from the group. If you have different dietary needs, you might have to choose a separate restaurant from others or restrict what you eat when you don't have a choice. Going solo allows you to be in control of your diet and your health-related habits. No explanations to others are necessary!

Adequate sleep while on a trip is critical to a good mood and thinking under pressure. If you have a roommate who snores or wakes up at 4 a.m. with her phone lighting up like crazy, you might not be at your best the next day.

I experienced sleep deprivation during my time in Iceland. There we all were in a large room with one long mattress pad. Fifteen sweaty co-ed hikers positioned one after another on the pad like a row of sardines. We didn't smell much better, either. And I was between two epic snorers! Going solo provides an opportunity to rest in a dedicated place (like a hotel room) to feel refreshed and ready to go the next day. And introverts know that private time refuels precious energy stores.

There can also be a lot of pressure when choosing activities, and it can be challenging to match the activity level of others. You might like a day at the beach but feel pushed to go on a rafting trip because everyone else wants to do it. I've even heard of relationships damaged beyond repair caused by disagreements related to mismatched budgets or transportation styles. Going solo means you answer to no one and get to be queen for the day, wherever you go!

Taking a trip with others means compromise, plain and simple. Being the captainess of your own ship removes the weight of travel companions' expectations and affords you many practical perks. You may be feeling nervous or not ready to go solo. After all, you have enjoyed being in the company of others on your past vacations. So, how do you know if you are ready to travel alone? As you answer these questions, consider your past travel experiences to help you determine if you are a good candidate for a solo journey.

Yes, or No?

- I've put a vacation on hold while waiting for a travel partner.
- I like to have a room all to myself.
- I like to rise early or stay up late.

- I have lukewarm memories of specific tours I have been on.
- I've had to change my pace when traveling with others.
- I have felt pressure to make sure everyone is having fun.
- I got tired of being everyone's problem solver.
- I've had a ruined relationship caused by a travel incident.
- As much as I love my life, I desperately need ME time.

Did you answer YES to most of the questions? If so, you are more ready to travel solo than you might have realized!

Whether you travel with others or alone, there will always be challenges in one form or another. While there can be stress related to solo travel, you can gain calmness when you choose to break away from the pack. You get to do things your way, in your own time.

Solo travel also builds confidence, clarity, and a cultured life. The world is a big place. As you solo travel, you may discover that your perspective of the world becomes smaller and more familiar than ever before. The foreign country, bustling new city, or strange landscape comforts rather than confuses.

Solo sister, as you go it alone, be ready to breathe a sigh of relief, confidently chart your course, and see how easily you fit into this big, beautiful world!

The Juice

Streets of Tokyo

It was late afternoon when I left Narita and arrived at The Prince Shinagawa Hotel. Can you imagine? A bowling alley and IMAX theatre in a hotel! The Japanese know how to treat their guests!

Once I checked in, I received an urgent note written in Kanji. While I marveled at the delicate strokes of the characters, I had no idea what the paper said.

I shrugged, too tired from the jetlag to freak out. The perfectly coifed young lady at the reception desk explained, "Change of plans. Please be ready for dinner at 6 p.m. tonight. Go to the lobby and show it to a taxi driver; they will know."

After a quick shower and a clothes swap to something more professional, I tucked the paper note into my purse and headed downstairs. The bellman called for a taxi. As I slipped into the town car, I couldn't help but notice the dainty lace covering the back seat. Such attention to detail! I handed over the note without saying a word. A quick nod by the driver told me everything would be just fine.

We weaved in and out of traffic along the bustling streets of Tokyo. It was dark now, and raindrops began to pelt the car windows. The driver stopped in what appeared to be the middle of a busy intersection and shrugged as he pointed to a block of about ten stacked buildings. He was trying to tell me the restaurant I was looking for was nearby.

I laughed at the absurdity of the situation. Dark. Wet. No umbrella. No raincoat. And I had no idea where I was. I hopped out of the cab and started walking. Within a few minutes, I saw an umbrella hoisted over my head, and someone called out from behind me: Kim San! Come with us. We found you!

This was my first night in Japan. I thought I was brave enough to travel here during the SARS epidemic but making it to dinner tested my true mettle.

CHOOSE YOUR HARD

A favorite quote from a solo sister: You can be lonely on your couch, so you might as well be lonely in Venice.

But not all women see it that way. Most women don't travel solo because they don't want to endure the feelings of loneliness that come from being alone. While no one wants to feel lonely, don't let the fear of feeling lonely stop you from traveling solo.

Of course, it is understandable to feel incredibly lonely after a significant loss in your life. Maureen, a friend whose husband died a year ago, took her first unaccompanied trip to Las Vegas. She told me she saw only a few solo women around town; couples were holding hands everywhere, and she could not get over the feeling of loss and loneliness. Maureen learned she wasn't quite ready to travel independently, but her trip was still fruitful. She might not have enjoyed it much, but she gained new traveling and emotional coping skills. I talked with Maureen recently, and she was traveling solo to meet some friends in New York City to attend a Broadway show! Maureen wanted to try again and chose a destination within her comfort zone. Her approach is an excellent example of slowly expanding travel horizons and confronting those lonely feelings.

Perhaps you have tried a solo trip and felt utterly despondent. If you truly desire or need to travel alone, it's time to try again! So, how do you balance feelings of loneliness, stress, or unfamiliarity with the desire to have fun and see new places? Based on my experience, it gets easier the more you have been exposed to these situations.

When we received military orders to move to North Carolina, we moved into our home, and soon after that, my husband went overseas to serve in Desert Shield/Desert Storm. I also traveled three hours daily from our house to attend classes at the University of North Carolina in Greensboro. With such a long commute, I left campus immediately after class, so I only got to know the local students a little. I wasn't home long enough to get to know my neighbors. Many military spouses said, "Bloom where you're planted." This philosophy applies to everyone! I learned that to enjoy where I lived, I needed to get out and explore my town and surrounding areas. And I had to do it by myself.

The other day, I saw a post on social media that I liked: Choose Your Hard. Solo sister, staying home trapped by your fears will be difficult. You will miss out on so many of life's juicy moments! It will also be hard going out alone, fighting your fears. But you get to Choose Your Hard.

The only way to find out if you can travel alone without letting fear take over is to take that first step and try it. As you are striking out solo, I encourage you to process your feelings. It's okay to feel what you feel. For most of us, these feelings are fleeting and will pass. Put your hands over your heart, close your eyes briefly, and breathe deeply. This way, you acknowledge your feelings (instead of stuffing them) and give yourself a big hug. Knowing about and practicing these coping skills can change your perspective. You are merely in a state of aloneness and are taking care of your emotional needs. And the courage that can come from this self-awareness and love will feed your solo superpowers!

The Juice

Camp Labatama, Bhutan Himalayas

What a girl will do to climb a mountain!

My tentmate is experiencing ongoing respiratory issues. Despite sleeping with my back turned away, my neck gaiter pulled up over my face, and my wool cap tucked strategically into the inside, I still developed a cough and grew feverish within a day. There was no dodging this bullet. Most of us at camp are experiencing gastrointestinal, respiratory, or altitude sickness issues. I was relieved that my GI concerns had dissipated soon after I left Jaipur.

One illness at a time. I didn't want to be greedy.

Oh, it is so bloody cold at 14,000 feet elevation! I slept with a hard Nalgene bottle of boiling water tucked between my legs. The next day, the same bottle hydrated me for the hike to the next camp.

At dinner, I ate with the heated Nalgene bottle stuffed inside my coat and warmed my thick-gloved hands on the hot herbal tea.

I brought a journal to write down my thoughts. It was too cold to think.

My top accomplishment on this trek has been continuing my twice-daily habit of braving the elements to brush my teeth. I brought floss along, but a girl must catch a break sometime!

CONNECTING WHILE TRAVELING

Do you ever get into your hotel room, lock the door, and body slam onto the bed with a big smile? I do! I love traveling alone and having my own space, and some of you, I know, are downright giddy about it, too.

But, sometimes, we all need a quick remedy to isolation. You can fill the void of being alone by connecting with yourself, loved ones at home, or others around you. You can connect as much or as little as you desire during your trip, but I encourage you to create healthy boundaries to take full advantage of the exciting places you visit!

Connecting With Yourself

I connect best with myself through creative writing. Penning random thoughts can be very therapeutic during longer stretches of downtime. Consider packing a journal, even if it is not a usual practice, and commit to writing down at least one line daily. I prefer a thin journal with a paper binding, particularly for rustic journeys requiring lighter baggage. I avoid bringing a keyboard and iPad because I want to stay in the moment as often as possible and watching the next episode of The Great British Bake Off is too tempting! I have no rules for what goes into my journal.

Sometimes, I write about my feelings, what curiosity brought me joy or calculate how much walking I need to do the next day to counterbalance that second helping of apple strudel at dinner. The gift of writing in a journal is apparent each time I revisit it. The memories and feel-good moments flood back into my brain and stir my soul.

Connecting With Loved Ones

The pull to share unforgettable moments of your trip with your family and friends can be significant. You miss them, they miss you, so how can you honor those heart connections to home and still preserve your precious solo time? Here are four quick tech ways to let your loved ones know you are thinking about them:

While waiting for transportation or a meal, send a fun photo or quick text highlighting your favorite activity for the day. My 98-year-old Dad was thrilled to see a snapshot of me swaying to Bavarian music at the Munich beer garden, although truthfully, he was more interested in the size of the pretzel I held.

The beauty of WhatsApp is that it's free, and you can record or listen to personal messages at your convenience. There's something about hearing a loved one's voice that makes all the difference sometimes! Share one magical moment with your family or loved one and ask them to record something that happened during their day. I got this idea from my daughter, a busy postgraduate student. She will send a message, sharing one fun thing that occurred during the day, and ask me the same. As with any new app, when you download WhatsApp, practice using it before you leave home.

FaceTime is another perfect answer to those homesick blues. However, check ahead about using FaceTime internationally because some regions restrict online calling. You will also need to observe time zone differences, requiring more planning. You get extra points if you practice your "I'm not having that much fun without you" face before you make the video call.

Conduct an internet search before you leave home for a foreign city to locate a post office where you can purchase international postage stamps. Then, select a beautiful postcard from a souvenir shop and jot off a few words to your loved ones. Send a postcard to yourself while you're at it. Think of how big you will smile when you return home and open your mailbox!

Connecting With Others

What about connecting with other travelers or locals? You can be as proactive or laid back about this as you wish. Remember, you set the rules!

When milling through a marketplace or lounging in a park, remember that others traveling may also desire connection. The only way to determine who wants to talk is to initiate a conversation. It can be easiest to approach a single person or a group of three, especially if they are waiting to book a taxi or group tour and need an even number of people! Before you know it, you may enjoy an enlightening discussion about a different culture or lifestyle! Last year, while waiting to check in for my flight out of Delhi, I spent three hours talking to a couple two years into their arranged marriage. It was a fascinating discussion and changed my perspective on the topic!

Remember that only some people feel the need to connect! Avoid uncomfortable situations by boning up on your social awareness. If someone is reading, doesn't look your way, or answers your queries with short, abrupt answers, chances are they are not desiring connection. Don't be that annoying person!

Signing up solo and joining a tour group can be a more relaxed way to connect with others. I used to avoid group tours if the itineraries were not an ideal fit for me, but I've changed my mind since joining a lengthy group tour in Southeast Asia. I filled my free days in the schedule with day tours offered by local companies to expose myself to more diverse experiences.

You can register for most day tours the day of, but if you want to guarantee your spot, sign up before you leave home. I check the cancellation policy to ensure there is no penalty if I need to change plans within 24 hours of the trip's departure. Before you purchase a day tour online, also find out where the tour picks you up and drops you off. If you finish a tour late at night and are surprised by the drop-off location, you'll have the additional stress of navigating your return to your overnight accommodation!

For those of you who are hesitant to talk to anyone, consider more creatively active engagements, such as signing up for a walking food tour, cooking, or art class. Groups engaged in creative activities naturally interact.

Finally, people-watching provides many chances to be amused and entertained. Consider watching local children play in a public park or observe street artists perform. Order a seven-syllable coffee drink and linger in a busy cafe or bustling town square.

Traveling is a fantastic way to connect with others outside of your world. And you never know where a connection will lead.

The Juice

On the Laugavegur Trail, Iceland

Who would have thought that signing up for a six-day trek through striking landscapes of geothermal activity, gorges, glaciers, and nature reserves would lead to new friendships that would continue long after saying goodbye?

And who would have thought these fellow solo sisters would invite me into their pack for more worldwide adventures?

Before them, I did not realize there were so many of us!

And we are unique.

We are the ones who feel alive and make others believe they can do anything because we believe that in ourselves.

We are the ones who understand what it means to be in and on the mountain.

We are the ones who push physical and mental limits while also holding space for spiritual connection.

We are the ones who embrace diversity and uniqueness.

We are the ones who make travel plans for years into the future!

We are the ones who hunger to take another bite out of this wild and precious life!

Solo sisters, we are the ones!

THE ART OF DISCONNECTING

For those of you who have had enough connection and dream of being on a deserted island, trust me when I tell you that the trepidations of traveling alone normalize over time. You may find yourself seeking solitude more often.

One of the self-indulgent things about going on a solo trip is that you can escape everyday commitments. There is no need to make your bed, do the dishes, or pack the kids' lunches. Imagine looking down at your phone. No messages. Now check your calendar. Free as a bird. It's just you today and only you. Close your eyes and imagine that for just a minute!

Seasoned solo sisters know what I'm talking about. You'll know when you are ready to disconnect when you bury your phone deep in your day pack and deliberately limit your time at popular tourist destinations in favor of off-the-grid locations without cell service. Your traveling goal is to get away from it all, seek solitude in nature, and connect deeply with yourself.

Early in my solo journeys, I enjoyed a packed agenda to keep my mind and body busy so that I had less time to dwell on unproductive thoughts. I checked my phone often for incoming emails, scrolled through social media, and looked up the weather in my hometown. I wanted to ensure I was on top of things at home and fought feelings of guilt about being away from my family! Over time, I desired more private time and less phone time. When I did some soul-searching, I found that taking time for myself was smart. After all, you can only serve others if you preserve yourself! We all need to refuel, don't we? These days, I relish disconnecting for days to immerse myself in my surroundings, wherever that may be. I feel total freedom and honor my inner gypsy!

I wouldn't call my desire for disconnection extreme, but others might because I often receive shocked looks when I share details about my isolated, nature-based adventures with others. So, read this chapter with generous curiosity and aim to strike a balance that works for you.

Plan for (Somewhat) Expected Needs

Before you leave on your solo adventure, you may have elevated concerns about those you care about. The key to feeling comfortable about leaving is to ask yourself what might occur in your life while you are gone. Is someone you love scheduled for surgery? Is your cousin expecting a baby, and does she usually labor early? Could your coworker be called upon to report on your joint project? Where can your customers or clients get assistance during your absence? The best way to approach these concerns is to create a plan to address them. Be sure to set up an email vacation responder so inquirers feel acknowledged. You'll feel better about leaving; others will know how much you care.

Here's what I mean: My dad is 98 years old. Given my dad's age, I was aware that something could likely happen while I was away. I am his medical durable power of attorney, so I make life-prolonging care and treatment decisions on his behalf. Before I left on my last overseas adventure, I relayed his desired medical treatment and life decisions to my brother. Then, I called his doctor's office and added my brother's name to the contact list in case of a health-related emergency. My dad felt secure, I felt responsible and relieved, and my brother was prepared to take over in my place if needed.

Plan for Unexpected Needs

A predetermined communication plan in case of an emergency is vital. This is as much for you as it is for those who love you. Because time zone differences can delay message response times, I check my phone for texts and WhatsApp messages first thing in the morning and last thing at night.

This habit came in handy not long ago. An early morning phone check saved me from a potentially dangerous hiking situation. The tour company I used to arrange my accommodations while trekking solo through the southwest coast of Ireland sent me an urgent message one morning. Met Eireann, the weather authority in Ireland, declared an orange advisory for

the day. Storm Agnes brought on 65-mile-per-hour winds, causing coastal flooding, power outages, and fallen trees. Cars couldn't travel by road. Hiking unprotected for seven hours was not in the cards that day. But I know myself, and without getting the text, I would have looked out the window, shrugged my shoulders as if to say, "That's not looking too bad," and told myself to give it a go.

Regardless of hiking in remote areas or enjoying a city tour, always ensure your trip itinerary, including accommodations, flight schedule, and travel insurance policy, is in the hands of your emergency contact. This practice is helpful in case there are flight delays or cancellations, or they need to reach you quickly in an emergency. Being accountable to others before you leave for your trip keeps you safe and keeps them sane.

Plan for Social Connection Needs

Tell the people you love what your intention is. Ask them what their comfort level is around your desires for disconnection. Work within everyone's comfort zone if you can.

I learned that my husband is on board with my desire to disconnect (as a pilot, he understands the value of compartmentalizing). My best friend wants more up-to-date details. Since I avoid social media and wait until I return home to post anything about my trips, we devised a way that worked for both of us. It's called

"Where in the World is Kim Now?" Since we were on the same phone network, she could track my journey through India and Bhutan using Find My Phone. And truthfully, I felt somehow that she was with me the whole time!

Otherwise, I limit my phone use to checking the weather and local time, calling local restaurants for reservations, and arranging transport.

National news can wait until I return, and if anything dramatic unfolds in the area where I am, everyone will be talking about it. I will be alerted accordingly.

Plan for Yourself

Plan to meet others but take a day to yourself. After my group trip to Greece, I extended my time there to include a solo visit to the Meteora World Heritage site. I enjoyed visiting the mountain-based monasteries and appreciated the solitude after a busy two weeks with others.

Disconnecting when you are away from others invites self-reflection and growth opportunities. It's challenging to create mindful space for your body, mind, and spirit in the busyness of day-to-day life. Solo travel, in its purest form, gives you that gift. And then some.

The Juice

Whistler, British Columbia

Standing alone on a suspension bridge.

Swaying between two mountain peaks.

While this can feel lonely for some, it brings me peace and connection to something greater than myself.

FEELING SAFE VS. BEING SAFE

I hear it often, "You are so brave!"

If I had it my way, I'd like to be called proactively brave, underscoring my panache for planning and preparing myself for safe solo travel.

You will have more fun traveling solo when you feel confident facing challenges or fears; that confidence comes from acknowledging and avoiding risks. So don't just shoot for being brave. Be proactively brave. This means making smart choices while planning to navigate your journey safely.

Feeling insecure about my safety as a female solo traveler was the first psychological hurdle I had to overcome and the most important one. I've had a few scary moments that have reminded me how important it is to be diligent with safety. Although I have learned that perceived fear is often unjustified, it is still helpful because it prompts heightened senses and a state of readiness if needed. Being hyperaware when your gut tells you to be diligent about your safety makes sense in today's world.

Last month, I drove 20 minutes from my home to Old Colorado City to support some performers from my storytelling class. Jives Coffee Shop was hosting several authors, musicians, poets, and artists to showcase local creative talent. What a cool vibe! Unfortunately, the event occurred in an area of town where crimes were rampant. As the night wore on, even though I was enjoying myself, I wanted to get to my car before it got dark. I knew I couldn't predict what might come my way and didn't want to put myself in a precarious situation. So, I left the venue early.

Years ago, this wouldn't have been on my radar. As I have evolved into a solo traveler, I am less naive and have become more mindful of potential threats wherever I go. In truth, you should take the same precautions no matter where you are, whether in your hometown or unfamiliar surroundings. If you overreact, so be it. You can laugh off your overindulgence for drama later over a glass of wine and celebrate that you remain safe and secure.

I talked to a male travel agent about the lengths women go to feel safe in a new environment after he shared a proposed itinerary for our female friend. He suggested she be dropped off by the public bus after dark and walk ten minutes to her hotel. I explained why this was too high of a security risk. Men don't think about this stuff; if they do, it doesn't seem to dominate their brains. For women, we religiously scan the faces of those who pass us by, looking for clues about who might be ready to steal our handbags and entertain fleeting thoughts of attackers coming out from the shadows.

I love that so many incredible travel blogs and podcasts are available to help navigate a trip's particulars. What I've found, though (which applies to life in general), is that we can have a fantastic itinerary and thorough packing list, but fear about our personal safety can stop us cold in our tracks. Don't let the fear of feeling unsafe keep your bucket list dreams stuck in the bucket!

At the end of this chapter, I share a journal entry that will take you through one of my most frightful experiences while on a nine-day, secluded trek. I include it because this is the reality of solo travel for women. I do not want to sugarcoat solo travel. There are risks that you must assume. My nerves were frazzled that day of my trek, and I felt trapped and out of control. Yes, proactively brave me took over, but I still shudder, knowing my fears got the best of me. I tell you this story to illustrate how easy it is to let fear take over when traveling solo. No one is immune! That's why a fear-busting action plan is necessary to keep you safe!

Remember, feeling safe is not the same as being safe, so take your safety seriously when planning and executing your trip. You may be casually strolling the boardwalk enjoying the sunset with other tourists, but you can still be targeted for a crime. I have learned that almost every scary situation is avoidable with some planning, a cautious attitude, and a healthy dose of common sense.

Be Observant

Pay attention to your surroundings, make notes of landmarks, and be mindful of people walking behind you. During my Camino Walk one early morning, a man started following me as I left Burgos, Spain. He didn't have a backpack or hiking sticks, so he wasn't a pilgrim. I quickened my pace. So did he. I turned a corner. So did he. He knew I was aware of him when I stopped, turned around, crossed the street, and went in the opposite direction. He left me alone after that, and I resumed my intended path.

Consider Your Environment

If your solo desires are more city-based, consider taking a self-defense course. Attach a whistle to your purse and keep your backpack fully strapped when traveling by public transport. Steer clear of situations that could escalate to violence. One early morning, as I walked into the city limits of Pamplona, Spain, I sensed something was wrong. The shops were still gated, restaurants remained dark, and armed men in flak jackets and gas masks greeted me. They warned me I was about to head into the middle of a Basque political uprising! I did an about-face. Breakfast would have to wait for another three miles. If you think you might be walking into something dangerous, turn around and don't wait for a warning that might not come.

In more secluded areas, think about how you'd feel secure if lost in the terrain or caught in inclement weather. I do a lot of remote solo hiking, so I signed up for a survival course and learned how to pack effectively for lousy weather. I'm proud to say that not only can I rock a look of head-to-toe Gore-Tex, but I know how to use ground signals to attract help and can confidently pick the suitable colored berries on a bush that will least likely poison me if I run out of food.

Think about the places where you will spend your time and create an empowered action plan before you go. Access to the internet makes learning about where you are going so easy. Preplan how you will get from one location to another and only occasionally reference Google Maps on your phone when you are walking so you will look confident. If you are taking public transportation, don't arrive too early at your stop. You want other passengers to assemble, and then you can join them. Better yet, start a conversation with the locals as you wait. You'll get tips on the local area and advice about where and where not to go. You can also download various apps to learn more about the area you are visiting and how to navigate it. For example, the Visit a City app shows you nearby attractions and their distance from your location and helps you create a plan for navigating independently and safely.

Be Watchful at Night

At nighttime, vulnerability can rise. Continuously scan the surrounding area and avoid dimly lit streets and dark parking lots. Plan how to get to the shopping area, hotel, or restaurant without looking too often at your phone for directions. Dine at restaurants near your hotel or treat yourself to a stay at a quaint inn or bed and breakfast offering on-site evening meals.

Choose a flight that lands well before the sun drops so you have adequate time to make it to your hotel. If you can't avoid an evening landing, choose a hotel nearby that has an airport shuttle.

Select the Safest Location

Research ahead of time for seedy regions of a city and plan to avoid certain streets or neighborhoods. If you're uncomfortable with the location of a bus stop or train station, that's the time to choose a more secure mode of transportation like a licensed taxi, Uber, or Grab. If you've booked a day trip with a local tour company and the meet-up time is five in the morning when it's still dark outside, stay at a hotel near the pickup location to avoid walking too far. I planned a tour leaving London at midnight and was happy to pay fifty pounds sterling more at a nearby hotel for peace of mind.

Know Who You Are Meeting

I've observed other solo sisters pre-arrange meet-ups online through social media platforms before they arrive in a foreign country. To keep it safe, if you agree to meet another woman locally, check their background through several online networks and agree to meet them in a busy, public place.

When you sign up for a tour, get the tour guide's name and WhatsApp or cell phone number. Send them a message the day before the tour and await confirmation. Ask them for an identifier such as a bright red shirt or Acme Tour Company van logo so you know who you are looking for.

Discourage Theft and Violence

You can protect yourself against petty theft or violence in several ways. Always keep your passport, phone, cash, and cards on your person and place some of your money in a different location. Leave your expensive jewelry, watches, or designer purses at home. In fact, why do you even have a designer purse? Shouldn't you be spending your hard-earned money on plane tickets?

A crossbody bag is perfect for most city situations and effectively thwarts pickpockets. Since I had cash stolen from my wallet on a long-distance bus ride, I am now committed to always keeping my valuables near me, even if no one is around! And if it's raining, your rain jacket should go over your purse to hide and protect your valuables and documents. You just can't be too careful. Solo sister Janai stated, "Yep, it happened to me. I set my day backpack beside my chair at an outdoor cafe in Florence, and when we got ready to leave, poof, it was gone. I should have tried to eat with my bag on my knees." Her friend Pam tried to console her with a joke, "I put everything in my sports bra. If they can get it out there, they deserve it!"

Most people keep their passports on them and store a photocopy in each piece of luggage. That seemed a bit excessive until solo sister Jaci told me that her friend, who was visiting a foreign country, left her passport in the hotel while she was out for the day. When she returned, she discovered that the hotel had a fire and her passport and belongings were not recovered. You can imagine the scrambling she had to do to make it back home!

I urge you to spend more money on safety and security measures and less on souvenirs. Hail a cab if it's dark. Spend the night at a more expensive hotel in a safer neighborhood. Order room service if you arrive late in a new city and want to avoid wandering the streets looking for a restaurant. Splurge on luggage and money belts that have hidden zippers and slash-proof straps.

Back-Up Your Travel Plans

I hadn't thought about this until solo sister Claire voiced her concern, "Only a few days before I set off on my first solo adventure for three months! I started thinking about what to do if my mobile phone got lost or stolen. I would lose my flight info, hotel bookings, banking, and emergency contacts!"

Now, I always keep a hard copy of my flights, itinerary, hotel bookings, and emergency contacts in my luggage. I make sure those at home also have the details of my trip. Set up your phone to automatically back up your data to the cloud. I habitually download any recent trip photos to an external hard drive immediately and then delete them from my phone before starting a new trip. That way, I won't lose those precious memories if my phone gets lost or damaged or The Cloud crashes.

Carry your phone cable, wall charger, and a country-appropriate power adapter to charge your phone anywhere. You'll be glad you did if an extra battery pack suddenly doesn't work.

Blend In

Consider dressing conservatively to avoid inappropriate behavior or unwanted attention. You want to mesh with the locals as much as possible. Look ahead at what the public wears by season and try to match the vibe and color scheme as best you can. If you are visiting a place that offers clothing at bargain prices, avoid the apparent selections that scream tourist. I cannot tell you how often I saw Americans wearing Thai pants with colorful designs from the night markets in Southeast Asia, and they stuck out even more clearly as foreigners. Disclaimer: I decided to buy a pair, telling myself I would wear them only in my hotel room and at home because they are so comfy!

If you visit a place where the lifestyle is far removed from your culture and understanding, avoid looking like an unaware tourist. Familiarize yourself with a foreign country's customs, including how to dress and what behaviors or gestures are considered rude or inappropriate. You want to avoid trouble with local law enforcement agencies, especially in countries with strict regulations.

Learn a few key phrases in the foreign language. Many foreign countries pronounce some understandable version of "American," so if you hear a similar word, you know someone is talking about you. Smile and nod like you understand the conversation, even if you don't. If you can't retain many languages, at least learn to say hello, thank you, and please in a foreign language. Notice I said YOU should learn some of the language. Not me. I memorized more than five hundred German words only to panic and have some Spanish eke out when it came time to request a table for one. "Mesa for uno, por favor." Geez. In disgust, the German waiter shook his head and sent me to a corner table.

Get Good at Half-Truths

I made a huge mistake when I was walking in Ireland. After a glorious morning along the coast, I was stopped by a man driving a golf cart. He was very friendly and started asking me all kinds of questions, and I just chatted away, telling him of my plans for the next few days. Toward the end of the conversation, he asked me to dinner. I am sure he assumed that because I was traveling alone, I did not have a partner. I informed him I did indeed have a partner and off he drove. I walked away in disbelief. How had I let my guard down? I vowed never to do that again!

So, don’t let your guard down. If someone asks, tell them you are visiting family, seeing a friend, or meeting with a group or a spouse. When you get into a taxi or Uber, make a fake call to someone, telling them you are on your way. That way, the driver knows someone is expecting you soon. In the past, it was a badge of honor to share that I was traveling solo. Now, I realize that claim can prompt an invitation to something I don't want. It's not necessary to impress others with your travel feats. It's much more important to stay safe.

Never tell someone your itinerary, no matter how excited you are. It can be easy to grow complacent when you have had a cocktail or had a day of fun and relaxation, so crafting a fake story ahead of time is ideal so you don't have to think on the spot. Get good at these harmless half-truths and prepare them ahead of time.

Always reserve hotel rooms for two people. Yes, you have a roommate. And the hotel staff should never say your room number out loud. Ask for another room if that happens.

If someone approaches you to help them, never go with them. Tell them your boyfriend or husband is nearby, and you will call him to help. If the threat is not legit, this might be enough to scare them off. Then, find security personnel to help instead.

Refrain from engaging in a conversation with someone who approaches you. Just keep walking. If you feel someone could be tailing you, look for shadows and walk in front of security cameras whenever possible on streets and parking lots. Consider wearing a wedding band or similar-looking ring, even if you aren't married. Potential harassers are more likely to leave you alone if they think a partner may be nearby.

Delay Posting on Social Media

Consider waiting until you return home to post photos on social media, especially if you live alone and are gone for an extended period. You never know if someone may be waiting for an opportunity to break into your car or home. I learned this tip from a friend who posted her daily whereabouts during her trip to Peru and came home to a ransacked apartment.

Solo sister, trust your instincts. If you feel uneasiness, act on it. You want to be around for another Instagrammable day.

The Juice

Journey from Kenmare

It was my last day on The Kerry Way.

All I had to do was walk out of the bustling Kenmare city center and head straight up a long, undulating country road dissected sporadically by a few lonely, perpendicular side roads.

This section of my day would take more than two hours to walk before I reached the southern border of Killarney National Park. This was also the only time I was familiar with what came next on my trek.

I had walked into the park nine days earlier from the north at the beginning of my trek. I had only seen two campers in over five hours, so I knew it would be an isolated place.

But I'm a bit ahead of myself already.

This story begins several days before, when the female taxi driver who dropped me off during Storm Agnes warned, "I wouldn't ever walk alone. Too many things can happen."

"What? Do you think a serial killer is going to be hiking The Kerry Way? They are way too out of shape for this," I joked.

She was not amused. "Well, you just don't know."

I softly chuckled, having heard this warning from well-intentioned friends and strangers too many times before. I tucked her comments deep into the "not gonna go there" section of my brain and exited the cab at the trailhead.

Back to my last day.

I wanted to linger and soak up every remaining inch of County Kerry, so I woke up late and leisurely ate my breakfast of eggs, grilled tomatoes, and potato hash. Then, I slowly packed up and headed out of town.

I meandered past pubs, souvenir shops, and the local Aldi. I felt a little silly using my hiking poles on the city roads, but I knew they would be helpful in the rough terrain ahead of me.

I was away from town now and the paved roads had turned to country gravel ones.

And then, just like that, he was beside me. I had not felt his presence behind me at all!

As he passed, I said, "Good morning."

"Morning," he replied without turning his head to look at me. He quickened his pace.

I can't recall when the "not going to go there" thought crossed my mind, but it did.

Why is he walking so fast?

Why didn't he look at my face when he passed me?

I mean, isn't that the polite thing to do?

Unless?

Unless?

Geez, it's your last day Kim. Don't let this ruin your last day.

Chances are, this is nothing.

But why is he walking so fast and heading up the road to the national park?

He has no hiking gear and no water.

And (remembering the taxi driver), like she said, you just don't know.

My instincts kicked in. I decided I needed to create a plan.

I'll do this (and I swerved my left pole toward his imaginary groin), and he'll probably catch it, so then I'll do this (and I swerved my right pole straight into his eye). I practiced the move several times, jabbing my poles into the air like I was falling off a cliff or something.

Yeah, that would work. It should work.

I took out my phone and snapped a photo of his back to gather evidence for the police—just in case.

I reasoned that he would turn around soon if he were out on his morning walk. Maybe a better plan is to slow down and wait for him to turn around. But what if he hides on the next downhill? No, I had better keep close to him to always see where he is.

My feet quickened to an almost walk-jog. So did his.

Damn, this guy's in good shape! That proves he can't be a criminal, right? How unfair is all of this? If I were a guy, I wouldn't be at all concerned. Why, why did I have to have so much estrogen? Why couldn't I be a man?

And why didn't I get a good look at his hands? I think you can tell a lot by a man's hands. I recalled him wearing dirty jeans and a dusty grey jacket, and I surmised he was about 55 years old. I'm collecting more evidence.

If he were a local farmer, his hands would give that away. If he were married, the ring would tell me he loved someone. Farmers and husbands wouldn't hurt a solo hiking woman, right?

Yes! His hands would tell me if he was going to hurt me. I must see his hands. My chest was thumping now, and I could feel the pulse-pulse-pulse in my temples. My sports bra melted into my skin, the fabric seeping with sweat. On the next hill, I shoved my poles abruptly into the pebbles in a feeble attempt to hoist myself past him so I could look at his hands.

What the hell? This guy is not slowing down! And he is not turning around! Why isn't he not turning around already?

Just then, a truck violently rolled up the road, kicking some gravel at us. The man looked at the truck and waved.

I felt relieved. See? He's a neighbor! He knows a local. Silly Kim. Geez.

Or does he know a neighbor? Anyone can cast a wave. Did he just do that to throw me off? The "not gonna go there" came flooding back.

Another 20 minutes passed, and soon, we would both enter the park. I had just begun to think I needed to turn around, head back into town, and start again in about an hour. But then, he made his about-face.

Now, he was coming straight at me. When we got close to one another, I smiled partially and addressed him, "Man, you're in good shape! Do you walk this every day as part of your morning routine?"

Did I care? No. I searched for clues telling me what I needed to know and how close I needed to bring my hiking poles. I glanced down at his hands. Soft, no calluses. And no ring. Ugh.

He replied, "About three times a week, and besides, I'm not carrying any weight on my back like you are."

"Yeah..."

"Where are you headed? Are you walking The Kerry Way?"

"Oh, nah." I slid my hands over my transparent rain belt that held my trail notes. "I'm just out for a morning walk. My friend will meet me at the top of this hill, and then we're headed to Waterville (the files in my mind quickly spewed out the name of the coastal town I loved so much). There is a B&B on the ocean, and we will stay there. She should be coming in the next few minutes. I just talked to her."

I'm surprised I didn't share with him what I ate for breakfast and how many bowel movements I had the day before. Geez.

Instead of a polite no, I had to answer with a detailed made-up itinerary. This was, of course, an ill attempt to cover my nerves.

I could tell he wasn't buying it. Rain gear, full backpack, sun hat, poles. Yeah, out for a morning walk. Sure thing, lady.

Mercifully, another truck came barreling by.

"Well, enjoy." He pointed in the air with his pale, thin finger. You'll see some ruins when you reach the top of that hill. My mother attended school in that building, and she used to take me up there as a boy. That's a little-known, useless fact."

We both snickered lightly. "Ok, thanks, I'll check it out."

And with that, he turned toward Kenmare. I did not slow my pace. I wanted to get away, and quickly.

He had referenced his mom. Ok, now that tells me he is a serial killer.

I don't know why I have such dark humor sometimes, but I do.

I kept my brutal pace up the next hill but didn't feel at ease. I turned around, knowing that I was higher on the road. I should see him, and then I'd know he was heading back into town and further away from me.

But I didn't see him.

What? I knew I was walking fast. I knew he was walking fast. But I had a birds-eye view of the entire road back into town. Where the hell was he? I ducked behind a tree and waited.

I stayed obscured from the road for what seemed like forever. If he were going to come for me, he'd be back this way soon. Serial killers don't have too much patience, I rationalized.

I waited for almost an hour. I did not see him again.

So, I decided that if I continued at my frenzied pace into the park, I would get way ahead of him. I stumbled over sharp rocks and slipped on wet wire mesh bridges.

I glanced behind me every few minutes. He really was gone.

As time passed, my heart rate slowed, my strained eye sockets softened, and my shallow, quick breaths were replaced with a long, drawn-out, deep, comforting rise and fall of my chest. I would be okay.

This was all in my head. No real threat.

Was I unfair to the man who was out walking? Harsh in my perception of him being dangerous?

In this case, yes.

But it is always prudent to think the worst about someone when you are a solo hiker, particularly a woman. It can keep you alive.

I am a trusting soul, some tell me. But I am learning.

The way I see it, there are two choices.

Let the perceived fear stop you. Or not.

And that applies to nearly everything in life.

FLIGHT WOES – BE GONE

I'm all about positive thinking, but when you travel enough, it is unrealistic to expect everything to go smoothly 100 percent of the time. Flights will be delayed, you'll miss your connection, airlines will mysteriously lose your luggage, or you'll forget your favorite coat on the plane.

And all these things can happen whether traveling with people or alone.

While these situations can be upsetting, it's crucial to remember that you have the power to navigate them. How you respond to a travel mishap is entirely up to you. In particularly stressful situations, I see no harm in a well-executed two-minute cry (complete with deep breathing and one heavy sigh) to move past the frustration and into the resolution stage!

If strategic, you can significantly improve your travel experience and decrease your risk of upsetting flight woes. Here are some tips for optimizing your chances of getting where you want with your belongings and mindset intact:

Start by picking out your seat, depending on your class. You can learn online about your aircraft's seat maps (which will be listed when you book your flight). From there, as an example, search for: "the best seat in economy on a 737 MAX-800." You will learn about seats with more pitch, equating to more legroom and comfort. You will discover which seats don't recline or which windows are blocked during flight. You will find out which first-class seats tend to be used for crew rest if necessary, bumping you into a lower class. Picking your seat for maximum experience is crucial, and you will feel quite clever knowing that you have booked the best seat in the house.

Avoid the last flights of the day. Flight cancellations happen for various reasons, like understaffing or mechanical issues. You can reduce your chances of drama by choosing the first or middle-of-the-day flights. These flights often cost more but given the perspective of time lost and potentially unintended overnight stays, you may want to pay for that built-in security.

Find other flights to your destination that depart later in the day. If your flight is canceled or delayed, you can avoid standing in long lines and waiting on hold to talk to a live agent. Just use the chat function in the airline app you downloaded before your trip (you brilliant solo sister!) to instantly connect with a representative who can help you change your original booking or do it yourself. I tried this on a flight out of Houston, Texas. I took a different flight that left an hour earlier than my delayed flight, which eventually required securing a new aircraft (I found out later). This tactic only works if you have carry-on luggage. If you aren't tech-savvy, make a beeline for the airline customer support center to ensure you can get on the earliest flight home possible.

Carry on your suitcase when possible. Prevent lost baggage by not checking it! Carry-on luggage protects you from this disaster, and most major airlines have online baggage tracking, so you can check the status and know when your bag is safely in the belly of the plane. With enough packing experience, you can eventually whittle your needs down to one carry-on. That is a day for celebration, my friend!

If you must check a bag, consider investing in air tags. If someone mistakenly (or intentionally) runs off with your bag in luggage claim, you will more easily be able to track down its location once it has left the airport. You can add an extra layer of security by locking your luggage with TSA-approved locks. Thieves want easy. Luggage tags can offer reassurance when you miss a connection and want to discover your bag's location.

Purchase flights with ample time between connections. One flight delay could start a chain of missed flights. It's better to lounge for a few hours at an airport than run like a banshee trying to make a tight connection. Think about how unruly your hair will look with all that sweating! Besides, even if they know you are coming from a delayed flight, the aircrew are not obligated to wait for you. Planes must depart from the gate on time or within a few minutes of the scheduled departure time.

Give yourself enough time for overseas connections - at least two hours, if not more. When you connect from one airline carrier to another, you'll need additional time for customs clearance and to claim your luggage before heading through security again. Be sure to factor that into your flight choices when you purchase. Even though the airlines offer a short layover from one alliance partner to another, think carefully before you take it!

Try to increase your odds of making your connection or securing an onward flight. Against my better judgment, when I booked my return ticket from Greece, I opted for a Lufthansa flight to Germany, connecting in 90 minutes with a United Airlines flight home to Denver. I rationalized that I knew the airport well and could make my way quickly if necessary. Upon check-in, I changed my seat from the back of the plane to row eight so that I would deplane rapidly. Although I had checked my bag to America, I was savvy enough to pack a hairbrush, toothpaste, toothbrush, and pajamas in my backpack for a just-in-case scenario. When it was announced that the flight would be delayed 15 minutes, I began to look at other flight options for the rest of the day into the next. There weren't any, but sometimes, this preemptive activity pays off. The writing was on the wall when the flight out of Athens was delayed by over an hour. Although I decided to test my running legs (and cast aside my care for wayward hair) to catch the connecting flight (which I missed by a mere two minutes), I had settled into the fact that I would most likely be spending the night in Munich. I quickly shifted gears, secured a comparable seat on a flight the next day, and made it to a comfortable hotel in Upper Bavaria. I enjoyed a heartfelt conversation with a woman from Ukraine at the hotel pub that night and had a brisk countryside walk the following day.

Make the best of a missed connection. You can brood in your hotel room or find a new adventure! Avoid hanging with travel trauma buddies. These people were on your plane and missed their connection, too. They can't shake the fact that they missed their onward flight and bring a cloud of doom to the conversation because they insist on rehashing what happened to anyone who will listen. At some point, you must let things go. Once, I found myself unexpectedly in Washington, D.C., overnight. I took the Metro from the airport to the National Mall and spent the afternoon visiting historical monuments and memorials—a vacation within a vacation.

Use your extended layovers to recharge. Grab a meal, unwind, or practice yoga in a quiet corner of the airport. Check in one last time with family and friends from home. Some airports cater to longer layovers and offer fine shopping, dining, and fun attractions. For example, I decided to fly into Singapore Changi airport on my way to Thailand because I heard the adjacent butterfly garden and indoor rainforest would be worth visiting.

It's easy to get distracted, so set an alarm if you leave the gated area or the airport for several hours to ensure you return in plenty of time before boarding.

Take a photo of your stuff. Since I always lay out my entire wardrobe and toiletries before placing them into my suitcase, I take a quick picture of everything I am packing. That way, I have proof of what I lost if I need to make an insurance claim.

Make your one personal item multifunctional. Small purses may be cute and fashionable, but it's wise to have your personal bag containing what you need if your luggage is lost. In addition to my travel documents, electronic devices, snacks, and water bottles, my lightweight backpack is my go-to personal item. It has plenty of room to store one night's worth of toiletries and medications, PJs, and a change of undergarments for the next day.

Check your items ahead of time. When the pilot announces the plane will descend for a landing, this is the time to ensure you have all your personal belongings. Be sure to get ready to deplane; everyone is in a rush, and you will irritate other passengers if you need more time to dig into the seat to find your missing AirPods.

Finally, as a public service announcement, you only make things worse by complaining to the flight staff or passengers, who are just as annoyed as you with travel interruptions and inconveniences. They are not plane mechanics, luggage sleuths, or weather wizards; they are doing their best. It's good to remind yourself that you won't always win the travel lottery and give some grace during these times.

And remember that two-minute cry.

The Juice

Seat 22B

22B remains empty, except for the wayward crumbs of a toddler's animal cracker from a previous flight. The cushion creases await someone to quickly whisk away the morsels before they plop down and settle in.

Once I've shifted to allow their entrance into the row, I wonder if we will speak of our best travel tales or sit silently. The exchange level will depend on them, for I am just as content to share as I am to keep within my thoughts.

No matter the length of the haul, my mind marvels at the physics required to transport all the fortunate souls onboard. Then, I say a little prayer: Please, God, if I need to die in a plane crash, can it be on the way BACK? And just as quickly, my thoughts shift to the what-ifs that invariably seep into my anxious consciousness.

Ralph Waldo Emerson, an American philosopher, is credited for saying that life is about the journey, not the destination.

Life's most memorable moments usually involve intricate details (regardless of whether they are positive or negative). The landing place is often regarded as a grammatical punctuation mark at the end of the story.

But a destination is necessary.

When you next gaze into the cloud-studded blue expanse dotted with jet contrails, ponder this: Something begs for you to get off that plush recliner and act rather than react, calls you to seek the glorious unknown, and cares less about how you get there. It just wants you to get there.

Without the finality of a place to consider, we are left wiping away the annoying tidbits, striking up conversations that give us fleeting pleasure, and worrying about what may or may not happen.

There is so much more.

BORED, SAD, AND LONELY, OH MY!

It's time for a reality check. I bet you've been bored before. Sad even. And lonely, sure, of course. And I bet you've experienced all these feelings at home, at your local coffee shop, or in the presence of people you love. So why would you expect things to be different during solo travel?

A friend called me when she was on her first-ever solo trip. She lamented, "I admire all you women who can find strength in traveling alone. I'm not good at this. I'd change my flight and go home tomorrow if I knew I wouldn't feel completely humiliated at my failed attempt to travel solo." I told her that I felt the same way on my first solo trip, and the worst-case scenario was that she had a hotel room all to herself, and she could stay in bed reading or watching television and take it easy if she wanted to. She ended up staying and having some fun but made it clear it would be a while before she tried traveling solo again.

The reality of solo travel, and indeed the reality of life, is that you will not be happy, entertained, or inspired 100 percent of the time. I want to encourage you not to give up. It helps to have a plan to meet these challenging feelings head-on.

Boredom

You may have some downtime sitting around in your hotel room. You've had a cup of tea and finished the last packed granola bar, and you have hours to wait until you take off for a tour of the city. You can start scrolling through social media or pick up the crumpled pages of the crossword puzzle book you stuffed into your purse at the last minute, but why not deepen your understanding of the city you are visiting instead? Perform an online search and learn about famous people who once made the city their home. Was the region significant for advancements in technology, medicine, or history? Listen to an audiobook written by a local author or find poetry, a short story, or a film that features the area of interest. If you have more time, plan an impromptu visit to the local museum or art district. Stroll to a nearby cafe and people-watch, searching to see if a passerby looks like someone you know back home. Or strike up a conversation with a solo sister sitting nearby! If you have artistic abilities, sketch a doodle on a paper napkin and let your mind wander just like your pen--without an agenda. Plan your next solo vacation if you are still seeking a distraction from boredom!

Sadness

While the excitement of an adventure or new surroundings can often provide a dopamine rush, you may feel disappointed about something. You may miss a loved one and wish they were around to share your excitement or something memorable. Maybe you feel self-conscious in public and believe others are staring with pity at the poor, lonely woman. They are likely envious of you because they understand you get to do what you want, eat what you want, and don't have to get an okay from a travel partner! If you ever feel self-conscious, I want you to think about this: Do you remember what the person next to you at lunch was wearing? What about the lady who was walking down the street by herself? What did you notice about her? Oh, you didn't even notice her? That's my point! Most people are too busy thinking about their plans to care about yours.

If you want to add cheer to your day, scour local city guides for uplifting activities, head to a comedy club, watch children in the park or at a hands-on science museum, sign up for an activity-based group tour, or take in a show. It also serves you to sit and journal about your sadness. You might be surprised by what comes from listening and responding to your aching heart.

Loneliness

Sometimes, a girl's got to find a friend! When you are ready for connection (after calling everyone back home!), get out and about. Now is not the time to succumb to decision fatigue and stay holed up in your hotel. You want to take action to fill your time! If you are an active member of a social media group, find friends who live in the area you are visiting and send a private message. If you both feel comfortable and agree, meet. What a fantastic opportunity an insider can provide you! She may be willing to show you the best parts of the city, meet you for a bike ride, or arrange a fun day at the park.

Use the internet to reach out. Search for group day tours or meet-ups with people with similar interests. You might find yourself in an enjoyable, spontaneous situation like Naomi. This solo sister had flown from Virginia Beach to Denver on a whim after she had found significantly reduced airfares to Colorado.

Without any plans and looking to socialize, she popped into our gathering, ready to mix and mingle! It was fun for our group, too, getting to know someone from a different area of the country.

Remember that the threat of feeling bored, sad, or lonely can steal your joy of travel. Decide to stake your claim for fun and adventure and take the necessary steps to create it wherever you are.

The Juice

The Casita in Cascais, Portugal

Celine met me in Sintra, where we meandered inside the whimsical, pastel castle walls. The tilework was so elaborate it eclipsed the rolling, green hillside.

Back at her home, I nodded to the gardener tending the organic terraces. The housekeeper offered me a chilled glass of Zumo de Naranja (freshly squeezed from oranges on the property!) and led me to my room through common areas embellished with floor-to-ceiling canvases. Celine had brilliantly mastered light and shadow in her works exhibited here and in Madrid and Copenhagen.

Eyes wide and shocked that Celine had not once alluded to her affluence or skills, I entered the guest room beautifully appointed in azure and cream. The sliding glass doors led to the pool and, beyond that, a steep hiking trail that traversed the cliffside before dropping to the edge of the Atlantic Ocean.

What a traveler's dream. Five-star everything for the cost of a plane ticket! How fortunate I was to befriend Celine and that she insisted I visit! And yet, something was wrong. I felt empty. I shook my head in confusion. Here I was, lounging on a plush bed, overlooking the ocean, in a beautiful country, and spending time with a dear friend. I checked myself. No, I was not jealous of her circumstance nor despairing of my own.

I took out my journal to write, hoping to find the truth in my loneliness. And then it hit me. She could not be the dear friend I thought she was! I knew she was not a boastful woman, but why would she hide the joy-filled things about her life from me?

Aren't good friends the ones you can cry with as well as celebrate with?

I will tell her this tomorrow, and we will make time to honor her work and life's accomplishments. We will go to the National Museum of Madrid, and she will tell me what she loves about one of her favorite paintings. We will walk briskly along the sandy beach with her hound, Max. And I will ask her more deeply about her grandchildren and why she paints the way she does. And then, I will call her a dear friend.

RX FOR TRAVEL ANXIETY

Ok, you are ready to travel solo! But you freeze just as you focus on one aspect of the trip that makes you nervous.

Solo Sister Maggie experienced this too, moaning, "Can we talk about self-imposed travel anxiety? It's so ridiculous. I'm planning a ski trip to Italy, and I've been outside the country before, so that's nothing new. Packing is easy, but my anxiety is so crushing when I think about all the moving parts of the trip. I'm almost paralyzed with indecision. The stopover cities, which transport to take, the day tour choices, and aargh, the list goes on. Why do I do this to myself?"

I know how I feel when faced with many choices and decisions that build upon one another. Aargh is right! My brain gets bogged down when I still need to finalize the bits and pieces of a trip, and I stop enjoying the planning process. All these little things add up and can overwhelm you to the point where you don't go on a trip or, at the very least, steal your joy when planning one.

If you cannot decide about some element of your trip, give yourself time to delve deeper so you have the entire picture to consider. Remember that the longer you wait to decide, the more overwhelmed you will feel with one more loose string to deal with. If you still can't decide, take a break! Wait 48 hours and commit to making that final decision. Sometimes, clarity happens when we free our brain to relax a bit. Also, think about a backup plan. If your original choice for a day tour, for example, is no longer available or gets canceled, you have an automatic go-to waiting in the wings.

Or, you can just say yes to whatever and figure it out afterward. This advice is for the chill women in the group. Type A's know better than to use this approach!

I was still contemplating an overnight train from Bangkok to Chiang Mai for one of my upcoming trips and couldn't move forward with plans until I decided. The 13+ hour route was one of

Thailand's most extended train trips, and I was told, "You don't want to miss the experience of traveling like the locals!" Those were the magic words. I booked myself on the sleeper train despite knowing I would still be exhausted from the 10,000 airmiles I had flown less than two days prior.

Then, I read that no water or food would be available for purchase, first-class beds would not be an option, and only squat toilets would be available. Oh, and dress in layers because it gets pretty chilly onboard. Lovely. I proceeded with my plans, not one to back down from a challenge. The thought of so much discomfort plagued me, though, and my concern over the choice escalated. I knew it was time to put my travel anxiety plan into practice.

Whenever I am tripped up by decision fatigue or having mental blocks, I follow this three-step plan to work through any unwanted anxiety, and I believe it can help you take control of your stress and your trip, too.

Step 1: Capture the Stress

Write down what is causing you the most stress on paper. When you list your concerns, your brain automatically compartmentalizes them;

you can tackle one item at a time, and they don't seem nearly as unsurmountable as you once thought. Using my train example, I wrote down: long train ride, travel fatigue, must bring water and food, cold cabins, uncomfortable seats, sharing my cabin with five other people, and no Western toilets. I was also concerned about disturbing my cabinmates if I woke up in the middle of the night.

Step 2: Let it Go or Make a Plan

Next to each concern, determine what is within your control and what is not and either let it go or create a plan.

For me, I wrote down:

Long train ride: I wanted to live like a local, so suck it up, Buttercup.

Travel fatigue: When I arrive in Bangkok, instead of going shopping that night, I'll go to bed earlier to be refreshed for the day I ride the train. The night markets in Chang Mai are better anyway.

Must bring water and food: I will purchase snacks and bottled water (or purify water from the tap) in the afternoon before I board the evening train. I will be close to food markets and have plenty of time to purchase.

Cold cabins: I will dress in layers. I will also be lugging all my stuff so I can pull out additional clothing items if needed.

Uncomfortable seats: Oh, poor me! I am going to see beautiful temples, lush forests, and mountains. Enough said.

Sharing my cabin with strangers: I slept with 11 Italian cyclists in a 12-berth hostel in Spain, so this should be easy. And who knows? I might meet a fellow solo sister!

Night awakening: I will bring a small headlamp, read a novel, or do crossword puzzles.

Squatty potties: I should definitely book a flight.

Step 3: Fill in Your Itinerary

Once you've captured every element related to your overall concern and planned for the items you have some control over, add your to-do items to your itinerary to remember them. For example, I scribbled into my plans for arrival in Bangkok, "Bed by 8 pm tonight," and the next day, "Dinner, then purchase food and water for the train and store in backpack."

Viola! This kind of well-thought-out plan addresses concerns head-on and will allow you to move on to the next phase of planning your journey. Following the steps takes a little brainpower, but that's a much better look on you than a frenzied face in a foreign land.

The Juice

Gleis 6, Munich Railway Station

As the train to Bolzano slowed, the crowds clustered closer to the doors, moving like a swarm of bees into the open doors.

We inched closer. I had no idea which platform area to access, and I knew we might have to walk through several long train compartments to find our reserved seats. I was laser-focused on quickly finding those seats!

Once inside the vestibule, I looked for her.

She was right next to me, and now she was far away! How did that happen?

That's when I had a flashback to the nightmare I had days before our trip. The sea of passengers had enveloped my daughter on the platform. The train doors closed, and just like that, I left her behind on my way to Italy.

But this wasn't a dream!

I felt a pounding heat in my chest and head and beckoned my daughter to board the train.

"Kat! Come on!" My shrill voice could've derailed the train.

I saw her calmly turn to the German woman next to her, who visually displayed disgust with my American release of emotion.

"Sorry." Kat explained on my behalf, "My mom's not from here."

Kat made it on the train, and we found our seats.

I was embarrassed because, as the parent, I was supposed to know what I was doing.

Next time, I'll have a better plan. This time, I will offer myself compassion.

TABLE FOR ONE

Eating in a restaurant by yourself is usually an anxiety-riddled event and is a big reason that many women don't want to travel alone. Short of selecting food from convenience stores, frequenting local markets, or rummaging through take-out fast food cartons in your hotel room, you must meet this hurdle head-on to enjoy travel and take advantage of global cuisine!

I can only recall once when I felt painstakingly lonely, and it didn't happen while hiking for days along the isolated South Irish coast or traversing the back country of Laos. It happened when I sat down to eat a meal at a small family-run restaurant in Viloria, Spain.

After a full day of hiking through gentle, sloping farm country, I checked in at my Albergue. Later that evening, I entered the dining room to find the other guests seated for dinner. The hostess placed me at a small wooden table smack in the middle of the dining room. I felt very exposed and awkward. I thought about chatting with others at a nearby table, hoping they would ask me to join them. But, as I listened for words in English, I could only make out noises produced by multicultural languages that I didn't understand. Not an American in the bunch!

I finished my meal quickly to avoid the continual stares from the room's periphery. When I displayed Euros to pay for my meal, the server waved her finger, "No." Not speaking each other's languages, it finally became apparent she did not want my money. I looked puzzled. She began pointing from one end of the restaurant to another, attempting to tell me that the guests had pitched in to pay for my meal. I swallowed and bowed my head.

In one moment, I was overwhelmed by the beautifully generous gesture and yet embarrassed thinking that the patrons must have felt sorry for me. I fought back the tears pooling in my tired eyes and walked back to my room, weeping all the way. I got in bed, breaking my vow not to play music while on my trek. I listened to Fleetwood Mac's Landslide and The Bee Gees' Stayin Alive on repeat until I drifted to sleep.

Even now, years later, a profound feeling of isolation washes over me when I remember that night. However, the feeling doesn't linger! I have shifted my mindset around eating alone and incrementally developed solo dining strategies to help me expand my comfort zone in this area. If you are hungry for a comforting dining experience, solo sister, you can employ these strategies, too!

Every strategy requires you to observe others around you and think about how you feel from when you enter the restaurant to when you pay your bill. Feel all the feelings and take note of the particulars. For example, you may find all eyes are on you when you first sit down, but within seconds, you are no longer the main attraction to others. If waiting for your food is excruciatingly painful, you might excuse yourself after ordering and spend a few extra moments in the water closet. Whatever you choose to do, be sure to serve yourself a big helping of pride for trying something bold!

Above all, give yourself some compassion when you are traveling alone! There may be times when you want to avoid dining without company. That is perfectly fine! Take a walking food tour or cooking class as a more structured way to enjoy a collective meal with others. Visit a local supermarket, grab a prepackaged meal, or shop the deli section for premixed salads and sides. Then go back to your room and have a picnic in bed.

The Practice Strategy

The only way to get used to something new is through a series of exposures. Even doing something once can shift your mindset and comfort zone dramatically. When you put yourself in a nerve-wracking situation and experience real-time feelings, you will have a much better idea about the extent of your discomfort (or comfort) around solo dining. You will probably feel awkward the first time you dine alone, but it might be better than you think. Practice locally. Why wait to feel uncomfortable while visiting a small cafe on a cobblestone street in Belgium?

Head to a neighboring town to avoid encountering anyone you know. The last thing you need is someone quizzing you about why you are eating alone. Conduct an internet search beforehand to find fast, casual restaurants before your visit. Quick cuisines like deli sandwiches, pizza, and noodle bowls are good choices. In bars and grills, avoid cooked-to-order menu selections and consider the specials. Usually, restaurants have these specials semi-prepared and will serve the dishes quickly.

The Distraction Strategy

My psychologist friend tells me that distractions can help us to self-soothe any negative feelings we might be experiencing. Have you ever felt a pain in your knee and then bumped your arm? Now, all you can feel is pain in your arm! What we focus on, we feel! So, keep your head down and your eyes focused on something more pleasant to avoid the death stare of neighboring restaurant patrons!

Try downloading and editing the photos from your day's excursion while waiting for your food order. Look up "things to do" in the local area. Perhaps you haven't hit all the hot spots! The classic distraction method of reading a book or jotting notes in a journal always works, but you could also schedule a video call if the recipient doesn't mind you munching in front of them! Be sure to tuck yourself into a quiet restaurant corner, speak quietly, and use earbuds to avoid disturbing others. Busy city streets offer people-watching distractions for diners who sit near big windows. You may also look for communal tables (popular in foreign countries and larger cities in the United States) and converse with a fellow solo diner.

The Crafty Strategy

Pre-planning is a critical dining-out strategy for those who want to tackle their anxiety about dining alone. When you think ahead of time about how you will manage the restaurant environment and use techniques that make you feel in control, you will boost your confidence levels!

If you drink alcoholic beverages, consider ordering a cocktail or glass of wine at the bar before you are seated. You will be more relaxed when you get to your table! Or ask to sit at the bar, often where other solo diners trying to avoid unpleasant dining experiences hang out. Do a quick online search of any meetups occurring in the town you are visiting. This is a wonderful way to interact socially and enjoy food simultaneously.

Remember to check out the atmosphere of a restaurant before you make reservations. You probably don't want to be seated next to snuggling couples dining on oysters and drinking champagne. Find hole-in-the-wall local places for what might be one of the best meals you've ever eaten! It is customary in many cultures, like Southeast Asia, for people to eat out for lunch, so solo diners are expected. You might dine during non-busy hours, like after the lunch crowd or before the dinner crowd arrives. Just be sure to check the customary mealtimes where you are visiting. In South America, for example, lunch falls around 2:00 pm and dinner after 8:00 pm.

The Confidence Strategy

Not everyone agrees with the fake it until you make it philosophy, but I must admit it does help to enter a restaurant with a big smile and a confident body posture. Greet the host or hostess by looking at them in the eyes, keep your head and shoulders back, don't slouch in your seat, and scan the restaurant as if to say to everyone, "I'm here!" while admiring the ambiance around you. Wear your confidence like the Brits don their fascinators - with pride and aplomb!

Be cool and calm. Sip don't gulp. Bite don't shovel. Suppose you want to be bold and show off your flare for independence. Order tapas (small plates) and slowly savor every bite while dissecting each unique flavor. Mindful eating is a beautiful opportunity to explore your palate and admire good food. Over time, I have found that during my solo trips, when I try to savor each bite, ask the chef or owner about a particular spice that was added to the sauce, or notice how fresh the fish was, I am met with sincere appreciation for my patronage. I have received countless homemade desserts or local beverages on the house. I always politely accept and follow through on my promise to write a Google review if I have found the meal or restaurant worthy.

For those solo sisters who are confident dining alone and do not mind company occasionally, I call upon you to look for those solo diners wriggling in their seats and invite them over to join you. Your compassion helps them celebrate their attempt to dine alone, and you've made a difference for someone in just one meal!

Finally, as you work to gain courage around solo dining and you need to add a light perspective to this whole topic, remember this story from a solo sister: "After spending 30 minutes listening to the man at the table next to me completely dominate the conversation, then turn to the woman and ask, "Where do you think we went wrong? Was it me?" I can say without hesitation that I am happy to be dining alone and in peace!"

The Juice

The Blind Piper in Caherdaniel

I waited several days for my first taste of Guinness.

Sure, there were other chances to imbibe, but some folks in Killarney suggested that I avoid the pubs catering to tourists if I wanted to experience a traditional Irish pub.

I hung onto this counsel for days, then stumbled upon the Blind Piper, a small pub in a small coastal town. I knew I was in the perfect place for that Guinness!

I entered a cellar-like room and threw my backpack and myself into a corner booth. The pub was dimly lit and decorated with antique gold frames and scaly serpent statues. Irish folk music wafted in the background but could not compete with the three locals at the bar having a rousing (and, I will say, most colorful!) conversation.

I tried desperately to listen to their exchange. The man with the wide blue eyes and tan jacket said something about a rugby player. The older gent in red and black flannel looked at the barkeep and spouted a bit of Gaelic in response. They all broke out in raucous laughter.

I smiled to myself. I didn't get the joke. I didn't need to. I was witnessing a moment of pure joy between old friends. Those are some of the most magical moments, aren't they?

I had drained about half my glass when a farmer walked in with his border collie in tow.

"Hey John!" said the waitress.

"Usual." said the farmer.

He planted himself not far from me and told his loyal companion to sit at his knee. The waitress plunked down a pint almost as quickly as he had found a seat, and she delivered the farmer's meal within minutes.

I looked at the farmer and his dog and smiled. "Lovely dog," I said.

"This is Jack. He thinks he'll get lucky if he keeps his nose right here," the farmer said as he pointed to his knee placed strategically to the side of the table. Then the gent went on, "Ahh, this is my favorite, roast lamb!"

I turned back to finish my beer. Occasionally, I glanced over at the farmer. He had finished his meal, and I saw him slip a morsel from his plate to Jack below.

I joked, "Looks like Jack ended up getting a scrap!"

The farmer replied, "Oh, no, not the scrap. Jack got the best bit."

And it was at that moment that I knew. I was truly in Ireland.

BATTLING THE BUGS

Whether flitting off to an exotic location or traveling across state lines, the last thing you want when you are on holiday is to get sick or hurt. And being alone when you fall ill means you don't have anyone to run to the pharmacy or local store to bring you an over-the-counter medicine or healing bowl of chicken noodle soup. If you travel solo, you must be prepared to care for yourself.

I added this chapter on wellness because I have a professional background in nutrition and health. I went on a hiking trip recently where my energy level and physical conditioning paid off. I ensured I was prepared physically for the weight on my back and the ascending and descending trails. I ate healthy foods and took my dietary supplements. I felt great and had a wonderful time!

Investing in your health and taking proactive steps to avoid illness or injury long before heading overseas or jumping in your car for a cross-country road trip makes common sense. Why would anyone want to spend a vacation feeling poorly or in pain and agony? Choosing the right trip and being physically prepared can help you enjoy every day while you are away, no matter what you decide to do!

This chapter includes my cumulative perspective on navigating wellness while traveling. Take what you will and leave the rest. Most of all, stay well so you can play well!

Breathe Well

Air Quality Index

Many countries around the world have questionable air quality. You can find more information on the Centers for Disease Control (CDC) website. I learned the hard way, so I urge you to take their information seriously.

While in Delhi, India, even though I knew the poor air quality index caused health hazards, I decided to tour for a few days without a filtering mask. I didn't have a history of respiratory illness, so I wasn't really concerned. The tightness in my chest on day three persuaded me to don a mask for the final day there, but the damage had already been done. Once I was back home, it took an entire month to clear out the heaviness in my lungs and breathe normally again!

High Altitude Locations

Living in the high-altitude state of Colorado, I've seen many tourists attempt rapid ascents to altitudes above 8,000 feet and suffer from acute mountain sickness. What starts as shortness of breath can lead to fluid in the lungs and brain swelling. You can't predict if you are someone who gets high-altitude sickness, so it's important to acclimate starting at low-level elevations before you attempt activity at a higher altitude. If you need more time to acclimate appropriately, consider asking your doctor about medication for altitude sickness. You must take it for several days before making your ascent, which requires preplanning. If you find yourself feeling ill while at a higher altitude, head back down and take ibuprofen, which can help reduce symptoms, but it isn't as effective as the preventative medication specific for mountain sickness.

Drink Well

In-flight

After airport security, you can fill your bottle with filtered water from terminal purifying stations or purchase bottled water before you board.

Avoid drinking coffee or tea while onboard. Plane water tanks are not often cleaned and can be contaminated easily. Instead, choose bottled water, juice, or canned beverages and tell the flight attendants, "No ice, please!"

In a Foreign Country

If traveling to foreign countries with questionable water sources, be hypervigilant to avoid illnesses that can sideline you for days with gastrointestinal distress. Avoid ice and blended drinks made with ice, and maybe not as obvious: use a straw instead of drinking directly from a bottle or can. I made the mistake of drinking directly from a can in India, and I paid the price for those convenient sips for a couple of days.

In Nature

Water purification tablets that clean water in streams or UV sanitizing wands are thorough and quick ways to make water drinkable and safe. If you want to be extra diligent, purify the bottled water you purchase, as in some countries, there are scams of getting regular tap water packaged to look like it has been purified.

Eat Well

Nourish for Your Needs

Think about the food choices that make you feel best at home. Pack snacks or find a grocery store for healthy selections if you are used to small, frequent meals. If you have trouble stabilizing blood sugar, choosing a combination of carbohydrates and protein can help. Try crackers and cheese, fruited yogurt and pecans, or granola mixed with nuts and seeds. If you are hiking longer distances or are highly active, your recovery meal should be high in proteins like lean meats, fish, cheese, tofu, grains, and beans.

While I encourage you to experiment with local favorite foods, make wise choices based on what is best for your health. Research traditional dishes in the places you visit to learn about the ingredients. Then, decide which favorites you will try or say no to. If you know you shouldn't consume fried or sugary foods, limit them. If you don't want to be experimental and love animals, avoid foreign foods that use exotic or domestic pets as a protein source. This practice is seen throughout Southeast Asia and other foreign countries where food resources for the local population are sparse. MSG is often added to foods in certain countries, like China and Vietnam, and this flavor enhancer may cause migraine headaches in some people.

Supplement with Whole Foods

There are many reasons why people only sometimes eat healthily when they are on a trip. Perhaps they have a rushed agenda or budget constraints. Maybe they want to forget about eating healthy altogether while on holiday. Sometimes I feel like that!

That said, your body performs better and can keep you from getting sick when you eat well. I use Juice Plus+ whole food, plant based supplements as part of my daily nutrition insurance policy year-round, and I take these capsules everywhere I travel. A few days of missing fruits and veggies won't hurt you, but if you take extended trips, especially more than one a year, you will want to bridge the gap between what you eat and what you know you should eat. This is especially true if you are in a country where you can't eat raw produce safely without the risk of getting sick.

Food-Borne Illness

If you visit a place with poor water quality, avoid eating fresh fruit, typically washed in local water. To be safe, stick to produce with a rind or inedible peel, like a banana or orange instead of a plum or berries.

Sadly, even well-cooked food can still cause an issue, so select street food carefully. Long lines are usually an indication from the locals that the vendor offers quality food.

For those who appreciate a natural approach to gut health, a yeast probiotic called Saccharomyces boulardii can reduce your risk of developing traveler's diarrhea.

Sleep Well

Jet Lag

If you've changed even a few time zones in flight, you have probably experienced jet lag. The more time zones you pass, the more challenging it is to adapt to the local time. For these long-haul trips, some people can breeze through the next day without a problem, while others are cranky, unable to concentrate, and tired for a few days. My best advice in combating jet lag when traveling overseas is to function as if you are in the new place already. For example, if you take off at 4 pm in the United States and arrive in Europe in the morning, try to sleep as long as possible during the flight to arrive ready for the day. It will help to bring an eye mask and earplugs on the plane to drown out the neighbor's reading lights or aircraft sounds.

When you arrive at your destination, consider taking a short walk around town followed by a caffeine nap. First, drink a cup of coffee or tea, then find a place to grab a 20-minute snooze. Set your alarm and get up when it goes off, even if you want to linger in bed. If you can't fall asleep, try a meditation app for 15 minutes or massage a small amount of lavender essential oil on your temples to soothe your nervous system and calm down.

Bed bugs

You'll sleep better knowing you aren't sharing your bed with bugs. Check your bed first when you enter your hotel room, even if you stay at a five-star hotel! Pull the sheets to the foot of the bed and look for minor, dark stains. If you see them, ask for another room. I remember Claire, a young woman from Canada who I met on a solo hiking trip. We stayed in the same hostel, and she took bed bug control seriously. That night, she went on and on about how much she hated bed bugs and waved the can of bed bug spray wildly around her mattress, pillow, and sleeping sack. Some of the occupants in the hostel thought she was over the top until they discovered they had red, swollen ankles from scratching at the bug bites in their sleep.

If you don't bring bed bug spray, keep and use the sanitizing wipes the airlines give you (as a post-COVID measure) to wipe down your ankles before bed. Bed bugs don't like rubbing alcohol. In Greece, as disgusting as this sounds, I had no choice but to stay in a room with bedbugs on my mattress. I sprayed mosquito repellant on my ankles, hoping that would work. It did. But next time I run into this situation, I will spray my whole body because those pesky critters traveled up my legs to find untreated skin.

Move Well

Prep for Activity

If you have an active holiday coming up, are you physically prepared? Training ahead of time for hiking, biking, or walking for extended periods will lead to more enjoyment and less soreness. If you have a regular exercise routine at home, consider packing lightweight stretch bands and practicing a few yoga poses each morning on your trip before you head out for the day's activities.

When I was planning to walk the 500-mile journey on the Camino de Santiago, I spent months breaking in my hiking shoes and walking the local trails with increased weight in my backpack. I also did daily stretches for my quads and calves. When I discovered that up to ten percent of Camino walkers wouldn't complete their trek because of injury or illness, I was glad I invested time in physical conditioning.

Protect Against Clots

Sitting for long-haul air or train travel increases the risk of forming blood clots in the legs, especially if you have a clotting disorder, are on oral contraceptives, or are taking hormone replacement therapy. Be sure to wear support hose and move about the cabin frequently.

Your Medical Kit

Do you need a medical kit? Suppose you travel in the United States, Canada, or your own country. In that case, you will know how easily you can get allergy relief pills, ibuprofen, ear or eye drops, toothache gel, sunscreen, sunburn relief spray, bug spray, cough drops, and other typical items. Pack health-related items you can't easily find at your destination or know you will most likely need. Suppose you have chronic headaches. Pop a small bottle of ibuprofen in your luggage. Experience seasonal allergies? Be sure to pack your antihistamines. There is no need for an extensive pharmacy kit.

However, my advice changes if you are traveling to a foreign country. You may need to pack something for every kind of illness or injury. Be aware that in some countries, common medications for anxiety, asthma, and even ordinary cough syrup are prohibited. For example, ADHD medication is banned in Greece, and sleeping pills are illegal in Singapore unless you have documentation from your doctor stating the medical necessity and quantity needed for your stay. While customs won't stop everyone, you don't want to risk a fine and detention.

The CDC Travelers Health website page can provide the country's official listing of banned substances. Before you leave for your international trip, search the internet for pharmacies or stores near the cities on your itinerary just in case you need to buy something.

Remember that if you need a prescription, obtaining one from a foreign country or the medicines themselves can be questionable. When I visited a pharmacy in Bhutan for a scratchy throat, I asked for cough drops and acted out my symptoms. Slapping my hand on my chest and sticking my tongue out while coughing and rolling my eyes around got me a prescription to treat pneumonia. Based on my exaggerated performance, I'm glad I wasn't carted off to the local hospital! Luckily, a physician assistant from America who spoke Indian (many medicines in Bhutan come from India) was in the pharmacy and knew the suggested medication was inappropriate. I was grateful for her advice. Unfortunately, I never found cough drops on that trip, and I now pack at least six drops every time I travel.

If you do bring prescription medication, keep the pills in the original packaging to help the foreign pharmacist know what you are taking.

This way, you can prevent drug interactions if you need to be emergently medically treated.

Although the standard mask protocol we used during COVID has fallen by the wayside, you should consider packing a mask when you board a plane, train, or tour bus. Truthfully, I am so paranoid about getting sick on a trip that I will discreetly change seats to avoid sitting next to someone who appears ill. If a seatmate sneezes and coughs all over you, you will probably get sick and get others sick. Cold and flu spread faster than bad news. Having a mask ready to keep you from touching your mouth or nose, using hand sanitizer, and frequently washing your hands can help you avoid catching a bug you don't want.

Country-Specific Health Threats

Vaccines

Look up the CDC guidelines for suggested vaccinations when planning a trip to an exotic location that carries the risk of diseases unknown in your country. For example, if you plan a trip to Southeast Asia, depending on your location and activities, you may be at risk for typhoid fever, hepatitis B, and malaria. Talk to your doctor or travel clinic to determine your level of risk and to administer the vaccines.

Consider packing a mosquito net, especially during wet seasons in countries where malaria is present.

If you opt out of vaccinations, your doctor may advise you to choose a time to travel when the threat of contracting a disease is reduced. That may mean booking your trip during the cooler weather in the shoulder seasons. Or consider an alternate location that doesn't warrant vaccination. Suppose you wish to take an African safari but don't like how malaria pills affect your stomach. Instead of touring Kenya, a high-risk malaria country, you may learn that you can have an incredible safari experience in some of the malaria-free nature preserves of South Africa.

Water Hazards

Research beforehand to learn about any advisories for swimming in freshwater lakes in foreign countries. Even brief exposures to contaminated water can result in infection. Ocean lovers, you'll be glad saltwater swimming is safe from these infections.

Travel Insurance

Most travel advisors will suggest you gain extra peace of mind and ensure your trip if you need to cancel it. Sometimes, travel insurance makes sense. Sometimes, it doesn't. How do you know when it makes sense for you?

A general good rule of thumb is to check to see if you are covered before you purchase external insurance! Some credit card companies give benefits for trip delays, lost baggage, and other inconveniences. Some medical insurances cover health issues abroad as well. I currently have Blue Cross Blue Shield and can research which towns in foreign countries have specific medical providers in network. I cross-reference the list of providers and clinics with my itinerary and make a copy for myself and my family.

You can also buy medical or travel insurance a la carte, getting only the necessary coverage. That's what I did before I traveled to Vietnam. The tour company I worked with wanted proof of medical coverage and repatriation insurance. I had foreign medical coverage through my current health insurance plan but no benefits for repatriation. This insurance covers the cost of returning my body to the United States in the case of my death. It was a sobering thought I had never encountered before, and I thought it was excessive. To lighten my mood, I joked, "Is it even possible I could die eating a bowl of pho?" About two weeks later, I brought it up to a friend who told me that she knew of someone who passed away while in a foreign country. His grieving family had to go through the complicated and costly expense of returning his body. After hearing that story, I decided to comply happily, knowing this was the right decision for everyone involved.

Whenever you purchase a hotel, flight, or tour, check the cancellation policy for refund amount and dates of inclusion. Write the specifics in your travel planner and online calendar for a quick reference. Some tour companies will reschedule for no or a small fee. If you want to choose between two similar VRBO or Airbnb properties or tour companies, select the one with the most lenient cancelation policy.

While we can't plan for every contingency, weighing the net cost of insuring a trip is an excellent place to start. To illustrate, I planned a trip to Wales and was all set to go when my shoulder decided it was ready for surgical repair rather than a hiking trip. I canceled my flight and received a voucher for future flights without penalty. The insurance for the tour itself would've been $150; the deposit I could lose was $250, so I made a $100 gamble that I would not need to cancel the trip and decided against insurance. I lost the gamble this time, but it didn't cost me much. However, if I had waited to cancel as the trip got closer, I would have lost even more money.

Travel insurance is less expensive than you might think, but how often will you pay for insurance and not use it? You must think about this check and balance to make a sensible decision. If you want the peace of mind that insurance provides, figure out what you need covered. For example, must you pay for flight cancelation or delay benefits? Most airlines will reimburse you even if you experience significant delays due to bad weather. As an added layer of security, it might help to base your decision on where and when you are flying, such as buying insurance for a trip to Florida during hurricane season or Chicago during January's winter. As of late 2024, the way airlines refund or compensate you for flight delays, cancellations, and misplaced luggage has changed, so check with your carrier before purchasing insurance.

Ultimately, decide what kind of insurance will provide you and your family with peace of mind and make the investment.

The Happy Factor

Don't let anything or anyone stop you if you desire to travel. As solo sister Zara pointed out, " My husband told me for years that he just wanted me to lose weight so I could do everything I wanted. I'm 250 pounds. This past month, I have rappelled, caved, go-carted, hiked, and swam in New Zealand, and then kayaked, biked, hiked, and partied in Las Vegas. The only weight I needed to lose was my ex. This isn't a sprint or marathon, just an adventure at my own speed."

Solo sisters, take your imperfect, perfect self out for a safe, healthy, and fun adventure, and never look back.

The Juice

Along the Camino Inka, Peru

Day two of the trek.

The trek leader said the key to surviving the next high-altitude pass was to "Not stop."

"No matter how tired you are, do not stop!"

Now I understand why it is called Dead Woman's Pass.

My thighs have never been so heavy. It feels like a literal brick has been embedded beneath my skin. My muscles seem atrophied because I can't seem to gain any strength from them. I only feel the brick crushing my thigh bone with every step.

I needed to rest, so I stopped.

Big mistake. Huge.

Lifting my rested leg to the next step was almost too much to bear.

I did not stop again.

Imagine what would have happened if I hadn't taken my Diamox!

THE MONEY POT

I can see you now: wriggling your pedicured feet, drawing concentric circles with your big toe in the sugar-soft sand. The palm trees sway to the tropical music bleating rhythmically from the swim-up bar, and the fruity umbrella drinks are coming nonstop. And that bold-colored bikini you thought you'd never pull off? Well, think again, solo sister!

Oh, no! Reality break. How are you gonna pay for all of this?

The topic of money is always touchy. Only you know why you spend your hard-earned cash, usually based on what's important to you. I'm not a spendthrift, but sometimes, I will spring for a premium hotel room if the location affords me the desired convenience or safety. Otherwise, you will often find me content in a more rustic accommodation.

Many in-depth online resources can help you create a budget for your next trip or find the best deals on flights and hotels; this chapter is more about how traveling alone can impact your wallet and travel style choices. There's more to a solo traveler's pocketbook than meets the eye. Read on.

Accommodations

Be prepared to pay a single supplement for most overnight stays. Tour companies that provide hotel arrangements, cruise lines, and bed and breakfast establishments offer these supplements to cover lost revenue from a second person. If you don't want to share a room with a stranger, you must pay more for the luxury of privacy.

Hostels provide a popular solution to saving cash, and many offer women-only dorms and some private rooms. Be aware that some hostels have age restrictions, so check that out beforehand. Many hostel travelers will be in their twenties, which can provide very refreshing conversations if you are open to it! Finally, some companies like G Adventures and Oat Travel, for example, don't charge solo travelers extra fees for some of their destinations.

Tours

Online tour operators like Viator, TripAdvisor, or GetYourGuide usually base their tour prices on two people. Upon checkout, changing the number from two to one customer doubles the cost. I've had some success contacting a local guide or tour company (you must dig online to find them) to see if they have an established group you can join without paying double. Be sure to vet them to ensure they are legitimate operators! I've recently found Airbnb offers tours in many cities around the world, so be sure to check out their services.

If a tour calls for a minimum of two people, the safest bet is to wait until you arrive in town and partner with another solo traveler who wants the same adventure or find another tour accommodating singles for no extra charge.

Transportation

As you become more solo savvy, you'll save a ton of money in major cities using public transportation like trains, buses, and subways. Instead of paying fifty euros to go from the center of Athens to the airport, I spent ten euros on a subway ticket for airport transit with unlimited city bus access. Looking at foreign timetables, street grids, and subway maps can be intimidating. If you get into a bind, rest assured that most people who use public transportation are immensely helpful, and many speak English. The more you use public transit, the more confident you will become.

Public transportation is a safe option for women who travel solo, but you need to be cautious about theft. Lock up your backpack and luggage, keep your valuables close to you, and avoid posting your real-time journey on social media. You never know who is watching and waiting!

The Emergency Fund

It can be incredibly stressful when unexpected expenses occur while you are traveling. You'll stay calm and make better choices if you have preplanned for circumstances beyond your control. Some of you might disagree, but "I just got to have those cute boots!" doesn't qualify as an emergency! Earmark the equivalent of $50-100 per week for this fund. This amount can cover an extra hotel night, unanticipated food and beverage charges (if you are expected to contribute equally to the group bill, for example), or a new rain jacket because you forgot to pack one.

The day I was traveling to a Crete coastal town reachable only by sea, the Greek ferry crews went on strike for 48 hours, and I had to use my emergency fund to hire a private boat to get me safely where I needed to go. It was a necessary extravagance, but instead of brooding about the extra cost, I fantasized about sailing the Mediterranean Sea on my very own personal speedboat!

If you don't use your emergency fund, avoid the temptation to splurge on something with your leftover money. Deposit it back into your bank account when you get home because another trip awaits you!

Tipping Practices

Before you leave for a foreign country, learn about tipping customs and whether you can tip using your home currency or need to tip in foreign currency. Tipping wherever you go is always at your discretion.

The hospitality industry is challenging at many levels, and staff are often underpaid and overworked, so you may choose to reward good service.

During a recent layover, I was served by a single mother from Ukraine who had a 10-year-old son still living there amid the Russo-Ukrainian War. She only offered this personal information after I inquired. Through the course of the evening, she provided over-the-top service. I tipped her accordingly. Later that night, I wondered if knowing about her circumstances prompted me to be more generous. Probably. But I realized it was my privilege to learn part of her life story. And herein lies a priceless benefit of being a solo traveler: without the distraction of a partner, we can take time to learn about someone else's life and potentially gain profound lessons, gratitude, or inspiration from those conversations.

Here's one more thought about giving out money. When traveling, it is easy to accrue a pocket full of change as cash exchanges occur. You may have noticed that many international airports have spare change donation boxes or that food trucks feed people experiencing homelessness early in the morning in large cities. Before leaving town, consider donating your spare foreign coins to an organization that helps those less fortunate. It's easy to do, keeps you from buying another airport kiosk refrigerator magnet or chocolates you don't need, and gives back to a place that has given you some amazing memories.

Don't Take a Trip You Can't Afford

It's no fun coming home with a bunch of memories and unpaid bills! One solo sister commented, "I'm leaving for a month in Costa Rica tomorrow and should be excited, but I've been mentally preparing myself to spend a lot more than I planned since it's the high season. I keep telling myself that the trip is exactly what I need, but I'm feeling stressed like I'm wasting money that could pay a month's rent and expenses."

There are two ways to afford travel: save more money and make more money. Here are some suggestions to do both.

Save Money

Going on a bucket list adventure could cost you thousands more than necessary if you put the whole trip on a credit card (unless you plan to pay it off immediately!). You will enjoy your trip and not experience financial anxiety if you pay for most of it before you leave. Wait to book until you have enough savings to pay for the required deposit and at least 75 percent of the total trip cost. Make full payment when you book hotels, tours, and entertainment so you don't have additional bills when you come home. Put a price watch on flights and be prepared to purchase when the best price hits. I've saved thousands of dollars on flights over the years by diligently watching prices for up to six months in advance rather than purchasing at first glance. Religiously use cash instead of credit cards to help you keep within your budget.

Make Money

The traditional way to make money is to work longer hours. These days, there are several innovative ways to make more money without taking up all your time. Why not consider joining the new world of travel influencers? You don't necessarily need to be twenty-two and look like Barbie! We are all influencers if you think about it. Do you remember the last time you found a great skincare product? Did you tell someone about it? See! You are an influencer!

Affiliate marketing is one of the most effective and turnkey ways to earn extra cash by promoting the products you love. I partner with an international nutrition company and suggest their products to others as I travel the globe. I get the privilege of helping others get healthier by offering them solutions I believe in, and I get paid by the company for spreading the word! The best part is that the monthly checks help me fund my next adventure! Amazon.com and many other internet-based companies offer affiliate programs that you can join for free or for a nominal cost. The important thing is only to promote the products and services you use and love. It is essential to be authentic! You might also partner with travel companies to earn non-cash perks like hotel stays or free dining.

Solo sister, with cash in one hand and luggage in the other, go have some fun!

The Juice

The Man from Munich

No legs. A mop head on a disheveled trunk.

Dirty forearms scraped along the street; his palms moved him inch by inch.

Four pocked digits cradled a mangled beggar's cup.

Filthy shirt and pants bunched up behind him.

It was hard to look. And harder to look away.

I walked briskly past him and back to my hotel, sat cross-legged on the crisp white bedspread, and ran the details of my return trip home through my head.

I zipped open my wallet and counted out the euro coins that jingled inside.

And then I went to dinner and tried to forget about the man.

The next day, after a hearty breakfast, I headed toward the train station to leave the city.

I thought again about the man.

I searched down the street, past the others sleeping on the sidewalks.

There he was!

I nervously dug into my wallet and scooped up most of the leftover coins with my adept fingers.

I cautiously walked closer to him.

Before I placed the coins in his cup, I gently reached out and touched his grimy hand.

I looked into his sunken eyes.

I wanted him to know that I saw him. I acknowledged him. I felt for him.

He said, "blessings to you."

I tried to speak but my throat seemed to swell.

I turned around to catch my train.

I stopped at the station kiosk to buy a sandwich for my trip, but

I had no taste for it.

I had two legs, groomed hair, clean clothes, and a comfortable seat.

That would be more than enough for today.

PACK IT UP!

I pride myself on minimalistic packing. I love to see how small a carry-on I can get away with. I blame the Camino for that. There is something very freeing about swinging your luggage around without breaking a sweat and not fretting over your clothing choices.

I frequently travel to nutrition conferences with my best friend who is a chronic over-packer. I used to give her a hard time until it became clear that she always had exactly what I needed every time I traveled with her. And this is how our conversations typically go:

"Geez, I wish I would've brought hair spray."

"Here. Holds without being sticky."

"I didn't get much dinner, did you?"

"I've got gluten-free, organic crackers and some olives if you want them."

"Ugh! I lost my earring back."

"I've got an extra rubber stop. Will this work for your post?"

"Seriously? Now you're just showing off!"

Based on these experiences, I've learned two things: 1) my dear friend is worth holding onto because, in the event of a zombie apocalypse, I stand a chance of surviving with her around, and 2) if you use what you bring, you aren't an over-packer.

Here's my updated rule for packing: If you don't need to carry your luggage very far or often, pack whatever you want. If you are the mule, do your back a favor and question everything you place in your suitcase. Packing just the right amount is a genuine skill that is honed over time, and you will eventually know what is necessary or nice to have for your own needs. In reality, there are very few things you could forget to pack that you can't easily find once you arrive at your destination. For additional reassurance, search the internet for stores near your hotel and check their inventory for consumable items you might need, like shampoo, sun lotion, or lip balm.

You will find thorough packing lists online for various types of vacations. I won't give you my version because I doubt most of you will insist on bringing a pack of twelve safety pins and some utility string for your next holiday. For those curious, I use the pins as makeshift clothespins to secure hand-washed undergarments to small string loops on a strand I hang in my room or balcony.

The best way to approach packing for a trip when you have limited space is to consider some of the most critical factors related to your travel style and destination.

Decide if you want to be fashionable or functional.

To be fair, this is not an either/or proposition. You can wear some adorable things that are also practical and convenient. You have to decide where to draw the line. For example, I wore a jean jacket on the plane to Greece (I get cold in airports), where I was hiking 80% of the time. I knew evenings would be cool and breezy, so I planned to throw the jacket on top of short-sleeved shirts matched with linen pants or skirts for a dressier night out. I knew a hoodie knit jacket could keep me warm on the plane and at night and serve as an outer hiking layer in the cool mornings, but it wouldn't look very cute at dinner. The jean jacket was clearly a more fashionable than a functional choice. The price I paid for bringing the jean jacket was to hand carry it each time I transferred hotels because I had stuffed my luggage to capacity. That said, I did get some gorgeous sunset photos of myself styling that jacket! So, based on your holiday plans, you will know how much of a fashionista you can afford to be.

Review your itinerary to match clothing to activities.

As you examine your daily schedule, jot down the main activities and how much time you'll be doing them. The first day is easy because you are traveling to your destination. If you travel far from home, you know you will spend much of your day in transit. Label the first day "Travel Clothes" and choose neutral layers that keep you comfortable from morning to night on any mode of transportation. These so-called travel clothes can be worn the day you leave home, arrive home, and any day that involves significant travel time. Because they are neutral and will go with most things, you can wear an item from your travel clothes allotment in a pinch (like if you've spilled red wine on a shirt and can't get the stain out), but I generally like to save these clothes for just travel days if I can. Travel clothes will feel fresher if you hang them up to air them out. Now, let's say you have a couple of nice dinners planned during your trip, along with city activities and some day tours. An earth-toned gauze skirt can be dressed up by adding a flirty blouse or made more casual by wearing a tank top and a scarf. You can wear that tank top with shorts when going on a food tour or heading to the park for a picnic and don that skirt and scarf for museum or temple visits (conservative clothing is required to enter religious sites in many foreign countries). Label the day you spend in the city and out to a nice dinner something like "City Style," and label the day you spend in the park "Casual Day." Then, pack clothes that match those vibes. The idea is to classify each day/activity with a few keywords that will give you a clue about what you want to wear. Finally, if you don't have access to an iron, consider wrinkle-resistant clothing, especially when dressing to impress.

Pick "the one thing" that will make all the difference.

When I planned to visit the Taj Mahal, I became obsessed with finding the perfect dress for my photo opportunity. It was a bright red wrap dress with yellow lotus flowers that decorated the neckline and hem. I knew I would only wear this dress once on the trip, but I justified packing it because I knew how special it was to visit such a universally admired masterpiece. I don't regret that decision at all.

Throwing a swimsuit into a suitcase (even if I have no intention of swimming) is usually a smart move, regardless of the weather or type of trip. Swimwear only takes a little room, and it is always nice to have the option in case a hot tub or pool calls your name. Your "one thing" may differ, but if you feel strongly about packing something, do!

Check (and recheck) the weather before you leave.

I devise my packing list about two weeks before I leave for a trip; that way, if I need to shop for something new, I will have time to find or order it. One of the first things I do is check the 10-day forecast in each major city I will be visiting. I write down the daily highs and lows, the degree of sunshine, and whether there will be precipitation. I also view wind speed for outdoor activity days because this helps me choose the right hat to pack. And then, about two days before I leave for my trip, I recheck all these elements to be sure the weather pattern has stayed the same. This second check can help you feel confident that you have packed appropriately for your destination.

Assess your need for personal items.

While you are away, how important is it to practice your regular skincare routine? Do you want to bring a complete face makeup kit? Some solo sisters I know pack very few personal toiletries, choosing to purchase body and hair care products specific to the area they are visiting. Or, if they join a group of other solo sisters that they know, they decide who will bring sharable items, like eye drops or over-the-counter motion sickness medication. Most likely, not everyone will need these items.

Should you take all your dietary supplements, or will the most important ones suffice? For example, taking calcium and magnesium is essential if you have osteoporosis. Conversely, if you get mouth sores when you eat rice and beans and the destination cuisine serves more bread and meat, you can likely forgo your lysine supplement. A registered dietitian or health care coach can help determine which nutritional supplements are critical to support your health care needs.

The same approach goes for medical kit supplies. Depending on various health risks associated with your travel destination and your most pressing health concerns, you will want to pack to ensure you prevent illness or can care for yourself if you get sick.

Are you okay with a more casual hairstyle, utilizing hairbands and ponytail holders, or are hairstyle items like curling irons and styling brushes necessary? Many haircare gadgets are available in lightweight travel sizes, so check out all your options.

How many pairs of shoes do you need to bring? This is a touchy subject, and I'm not about to come between you and your bedazzled sandals! If you are packing a large suitcase and have room, you can bring as many shoes as you want (within reason)! Most subject experts suggest choosing your first pair of shoes based on scheduled physical activities (such as boots for hiking and water shoes for snorkeling). Select your second pair based on road conditions (think how your feet will feel after trodding along all day on city sidewalks, cobbled streets, or dirt roads). Then consider a third pair for resting your feet and padding around the hotel, like a ballet flat or arch-supporting sandals. From there, ask yourself how important it is to take those black stiletto heels.

Choose organizational items carefully.

Decide if packing cubes makes sense. Hint: They do! I only understood the hoopla around packing cubes once I tried them. Before, I used compression plastic bags to remove air and bulk from clothing to increase space in my suitcase. The zippered compression cubes do the same thing, but the top-load zipper system makes it much easier to locate and remove a specific item without repacking everything. Investing in high-quality, durable compression cubes is vital because you won't tear the fabric when tugging and pulling the zippers to close.

Here are my organizational must-haves for every trip. All items lay flat and can be tucked inside the outside pocket of your suitcase or backpack:

Ziplock bags

Ziplock bags are great for collecting rocks or seashells, stowing lunch crafted from buffet breakfast items, or sealing a container of liquid that tends to leak. Choose freezer vs. storage for a slightly stronger bag.

Garbage bag

It's a good idea to have a bag for dirty garments. You don't want to mix smelly clothes with nonsmelly clothes! Plus, a garbage bag can house wet items during transport until you can hang them out to dry or separate muddy hiking boots or shoes from the rest of your items.

Foldable, lightweight duffle bag

Carry-on packing leaves little room for souvenirs or other purchases, so a duffle bag can be helpful if you have extra clothes or gifts to take home. This means checking your regular carry-on and taking the duffle and small personal item onboard. Be sure your duffle bag has reinforced seams or take on a sewing project and double stitch the seams to ensure a strong hold that will secure weightier items.

Drawstring cinch bag

There always seems to be a reason for a tote bag. A medium cinch bag holds your beach items like sunscreen and snorkel gear or picnic gear like utensils, napkins, and paper plates. I like the drawstring so I can sling the bag over my shoulder, keeping both hands free to carry other desired items like a margarita or glass of wine! A drawstring cinch bag also doubles as a daypack when you want to go out for a brief hike.

Check airline requirements.

Check all carriers you will be using for flights and get familiar with their requirements for liquids (especially European regulations regarding packed liquids), dimensions for carry-on and personal items, and maximum weight and dimensions allowed for checked baggage. You will pay more than you want to for exceeding size and volume restrictions. Only some airlines strictly reinforce their rules, but why take the chance? Wouldn't you rather spend your hard-earned money on something fun?

Do a test run.

Once you have a list of everything you want to pack and have selected the perfect-sized luggage, place every item on your bed and eyeball for redundancies. Adjust and then pack everything up. I mean everything so there will be no surprises on the day you leave. Make more adjustments if needed.

The Juice

The Dress, The Photo, and The Taj Mahal

A month before I left for India, I attended a lecture on the environmental impact of pollution. The presenter happened to be from Delhi, India.

I learned that the air quality in Delhi is the worst of any major city in the World.

It's estimated that two million Indian people per year die because of air pollution.

And I experienced these effects first-hand when I developed lingering respiratory issues for weeks after I left India.

But what does air pollution have to do with the Taj? And with my beautiful dress?

The Taj Mahal: This breathtaking mausoleum's color magically changes from soft white to light yellow to pale blue throughout the day, depending on how the sun hits it. Sadly, over time, the air pollution has been so intense that the marble of this iconic monument to love is slowly oxidizing. The Taj is now more yellow than white.

I can't do much about that. Or can I?

Moving on to the dress: Knowing that visiting the Taj was a once-in-a-lifetime experience, I had been searching online for the perfect, no-expenses-spared dress.

I wanted my photo to be very Instagrammable!

But once I learned that old clothing goes directly into landfills and releases gas and chemicals into the air, soil, and groundwater, I decided NOT to contribute to pollution. I would opt to keep one piece of clothing out of the landfill!

I walked into a consignment shop and told the clerk, "I doubt you have this, but I am looking for a bright red dress. It must be very lightweight because it will be about one hundred degrees where I am going. It needs to cover my legs and shoulders because I am going to a place that commands respect. Ideally, it would have a design that imparts the flavors of India. Hearing myself share these criteria, I laughed at the absurdity of my specific order.

The clerk smiled wryly, walked over to an overstuffed, round rack, and pulled out a dress that fit the description and me perfectly! I could not believe it!

I walked out of the shop with the garment in hand, $20 poorer but so much richer for knowing I had done my part to protect the environment.

And somehow, I felt I had protected the Taj as well.

THE TRAVEL BLUES

Until I read about post-travel blues, I thought something was wrong with me when I noticed a disturbing pattern. After finishing a trip, I would daydream about staying a few more days on departure mornings. I regretted booking my return date too soon. I was not ready to leave yet! I would return home to my routine, doing the same things repeatedly. I'd make a grocery list and do laundry. I'd resume the exercise routine that I swore I'd do every day I was gone. Somehow, that part rarely got integrated into my trip itinerary.

Adventurous souls seek novelty. The prospect of experiencing different things when we travel sparks our joy and energy. Back home, there is much less excitement, anticipation, and mystery of what the next day might bring. I've talked with other solo sisters, who agree that post-travel blues can hit hard and make you feel guilty for not having the best attitude of gratitude. Those feelings of sadness or disappointment aren't just about missing exotic destinations or new experiences; they're a sign of how much your journey meant to you.

I love everything about traveling, even the not-so-exciting parts. I will enjoy the trip long before I take it! It brings me joy to plan an entire trip by researching new countries to explore, putting together transportation plans, finding the perfect accommodations, scrolling through ideas for side trips and day tours, and everything in between.

Then, when I arrive at my destination, I lose myself in my itinerary and usually add some off-the-cuff adventures here and there just for more excitement. I take tons of photos to relive the moments later. I also write in a journal about the day's events and take note of any highlights. I don't waste time or energy posting on social media while traveling. That is an activity that cuts into my immersive travel experience.

Once home, my cure for post-travel blues starts when I walk into my home. I put my luggage down, look around my house, and praise the things I feel grateful for: my family, my firm bed, my hot shower, my views of Pikes Peak and meandering deer, and wow, none of my plants died! I return to my walking and exercise routine as quickly as possible because this is my investment to remain strong and healthy for future travel. We visit my favorite restaurant for a welcome-home Mexican feast and a margarita. I always seem to crave this cuisine no matter where I travel!

I select only the best, most representative photos to keep and show others. I thoughtfully post one or two pictures daily instead of barraging others with a photo dump. My greatest joy comes from sharing my favorite trip stories with my family and close friends. I deliver any trinkets purchased while traveling and enjoy receiving feedback from the recipients. Part of the fun of shopping on a trip is locating the gift item I had in mind for someone. In case you're wondering, one of the best questions to ask someone after they get you a gift is, "What made you decide to get me this?" A heartfelt conversation is sure to ensue. I attend travel meet-ups and talk with members of my travel group, where I get to share my experiences and learn about new experiences from them.

And once I have fully reintegrated into the regularity of daily life, I think about the next trip or look at ideas of where to go next.

Many solo sisters do not let the post-travel blues get to them and have found interesting ways to feel good and savor every moment of their trips. These ideas may help you feel better after your solo travels:

Break up your home routine.

Do something that gets you excited, no matter how small. Take a pottery or sketching class, go for a bike ride, hang out at the local coffee shop, and people-watch.

Do an assessment.

Write down a list of the risks and opportunities taken on the last trip. As you read your notes, take time and process how brave and proud you should feel for jumping outside the familiar and into the unknown.

Un-Solo.

Add in some people-ing (the opposite of soloing). Invite a friend to the theatre, volunteer in your community, take a relative out to lunch, or find a new meet-up event to add to your calendar.

Make a photo book.

Share your photos when you return home by assembling a photo book of your trip. Invite your family and friends to a post-trip party, where you can hand out small souvenirs and share your favorite travel stories. If co-workers ask to see pictures from your trip, invite them to lunch and rehash your adventures! When the day comes that you are no longer able to travel, you can spend your days going through your books and reliving every trip.

Get artsy.

Review your travel diary and look at any sketches you included to remind you to be grateful, relive your favorite moments, and enjoy all the good feelings.

Find a group.

Search social media groups focusing on travel interests. Envision a new group of buddies worldwide who will inspire and cheer you on. It always helps to feel a sense of belonging with people who share your interests.

Write something.

Start a blog for your memories. Send the link to

anyone interested in learning more about your travels. Be sure to insert some photos.

Decorate your home.

Print your favorite photo pictures on canvas and decorate your walls. Using acrylics, watercolors, or colored pencils, paint a memory from your trip on canvas or paper. Even if you don't intend to show your artwork to anyone or display it, you will gain hours of pleasure recreating a favorite scene.

Spend time in the kitchen.

Expand your culinary chops and bake or cook a favorite food you enjoyed while traveling to a unique region of the world.

Post-travel blues remind us that we have an opportunity to redirect our good energy back home. I have started to wonder if we spend so much time moving forward onto the next thing that we don't take the time to appreciate what we have just experienced. The answer involves something other than planning the next trip. The cure for post-travel blues is knowing that the juice in life is never far away. You can cultivate it anytime, anywhere.

The Juice

Samaria Gorge, Greece

It was pitch black outside. Breakfast would have to wait, but I couldn't.

I shut the door of my hotel room quietly so as not to disturb sleeping neighbors, placed my headlamp over my tangled hair, and adjusted the light to hit the floor ahead. It was less than two miles to the ranger station and the southern entrance of Samaria Gorge. I wasn't crazy about walking in the dark, but I needed to reach the entrance right at the opening. Besides, Crete has no predatory animals, and I had walked through this section the night before.

I had been anticipating hiking this crowning jewel of Crete since I arrived in Greece. The Samaria Gorge is reported to be the longest in Europe (total length is almost ten miles) and features sheer walls of buckled rock and Mediterranean pine and cypress forests.

Knowing I had to catch a ferry at 11:30 am from Agia Roumeli, I could not waste any time. Based on my time constraint, I knew I had to move fast and would be lucky to get halfway through the gorge and see only some of the ancient ruins and churches spread throughout.

Once inside, the sky slowly lit up, the sun illuminated the tops of the gorge walls, and I marveled at the spectacular views. I slowed down only to capture the most impressive sights, which never seemed to stop cropping up. I needed to run-walk intermittently to reach the abandoned stone village and Church of Osia Maria. They were worth the hurry. After spending a few minutes inside the 15th-century church, I turned around and hurried down the rocky trail back to my starting point.

With 25 minutes to spare, I purchased my ferry ticket and ordered a quick egg and toast. My body and mind slowed as I ate breakfast, and I reviewed my morning's feat. Impressive timing! Impressive gorge! But impressive memories? Not quite. In my quest to see this spectacular site, I rushed through it. To be fair, I didn't have another choice. The gorge was closed the day before, so I only had this one day to walk through it before I needed to get to Loutro for my planned departure home.

Here's another lesson about traveling blues: You sometimes get a different experience than you dream about. Perhaps it's just a spiritual plan that will prompt you to return and try again.

BUILD A BETTER BUCKET LIST

I heard once that we are less likely to make a bucket list for travel as we get older, which implies that we have dreams early on in life and don't allow ourselves to dream as we age. I must disagree, and when talking with solo sisters worldwide, they are on board with me.

It's true that when we are younger, we create dreams around our perceived unlimited potential. We might tell ourselves, "Someday, I'll go on an African safari or visit Morrocco!" Some of you make that happen early on. But many of us get busy completing our educational endeavors, working full-time, and raising a family. Reality takes over, and those ambitious travel dreams go on hold.

Delaying bucket list travel was undoubtedly the case for my friend, a top-producing realtor in town. Over lunch, she excitedly told me she would finally have an opportunity to go to Thailand and couldn't wait to see the elephant sanctuary. We shook our heads in irony that I would arrive in Bangkok the day after she left! But she was equally surprised that, upon reflection, she realized that she had not been on a trip overseas for decades.

When we get older and have more resources and time to enjoy travel, many of us dig into that bucket list of dreams, hoping to take a few lifetime trips! And if we enjoy traveling, we get inspired to add new destinations to our list. So, bucket lists can be ever-evolving and are for everyone at any age!

When it comes to bucket list trips, I caution you to recognize that trips only provide fleeting happiness. This can be especially true if you care more about checking off the next item on your list than profoundly enjoying one destination at a time.

Please invest serious time and effort when adding to your ongoing bucket list to create fulfilling travel experiences. I love reflecting on and reliving parts of my trips. Years after a trip, I can close my eyes and picture a defining moment, and my entire being lights up at the memory. For me, a better bucket list isn't about quantity but quality. Meaningful, all the way down to my toes, quality. And I want that for you, too!

With more than one lifetime's worth of destinations to experience, the guidance in this chapter can help you narrow down your options and help you build a list of trips that stir your body, mind, and soul!

Discover Your Why

Before you flip through a travel magazine or talk to a travel agent, clarify why you want to go to a particular place and ensure this destination offers activities and an ambiance that honors your values and reflects your core needs. For example, my return from Greece fell on my birthday this year, and I didn't want to be flying all day to commemorate my special day. Instead, I delayed my trip back home. I booked a tour to Meteora, where I experienced a magical day of visiting Byzantine monasteries perched atop high cliffs, surrounded by surreal landscapes. It was a perfect way to celebrate the blessings of my life.

PJ, a solo sister, asked our group, "I'm separating from my husband of 30 years. I haven't vacationed alone and am looking for a great place to escape, find time to think, and have some fun in the sun. Any suggestions?" The best advice came from solo sister Carrie, who suggested that PJ "dial in a bit more" because there would be a thousand answers to that question. Someone even suggested viewing the movie Eat, Pray, Love for inspiration.

Your generic reason for traveling might be "To get away from it all for a little while." But I encourage you to dig a bit deeper. Why do you want to get away? Are you someone who puts your own needs aside for others? If so, indulge in a California coastal yoga retreat or enjoy a European spa for refueling and pampering. Perhaps you want to get away because you feel discouraged about your life and need to gain an attitude of gratitude and regain perspective. In this case, you might choose a trip with a volunteer or community-based activity in Honduras or Mexico. Figure out what is going to feed your spirit.

Determine Your Top Destinations

Once you know why you want to go on a trip, it's time to make your list come alive. If you want to go solo but are relatively new to the practice, choose a destination closer to home. You can continually expand down the road. If you are a well-traveled solo sister, now might be the time to visit exotic or off-the-beaten-path locations! List five locations, ten if you prefer to travel more often. The idea here is to stay calm with all the choices; it's more about consolidating trip ideas to consider over the next several years.

Find the Optimal Time to Go (For You)

Conduct an internet search for the best time of year to visit each location. Summer might be the most popular time to head to Greece, but the cooler shoulder seasons offer the advantage of quieter crowds and better hiking weather. If you want to hit the beaches and swim to your heart's content, July might be the best month! Can you see why it's essential to know why you want to go on a trip in the first place? Your why will determine not only the places you visit but the season in which you travel!

You must prioritize your trips if the best times to visit your destinations are in the same season. For example, I wanted to hike in Lake Tahoe, South Africa, and Scotland. My research revealed that I'd catch the vibrant blooms on the trails in Tahoe in early June. June was also the perfect time to visit the mountains of

KwaZulu Natal and add on a safari in Kruger National Park. Scotland was best in June, too, to avoid the midges and crowds on the trail with the warmer weather. These findings meant that I needed to extend my travel calendar for three years to ensure I could travel at my optimal time to all these destinations. If the places you want to visit offer excellent visiting opportunities throughout the year, you can be more flexible and plan two or three trips per year!

Take Advice Cautiously

No one knows what you like to do more than you. And if you don't know, traveling solo is your chance to find out! If someone told me that I shouldn't miss the Phare circus in Cambodia, I wouldn't take heed. No matter how beautiful their costumes are, I do not enjoy watching people dangerously hovering in the air! Once you know if you appreciate a flashy show, walk through nature, or anything in between, you can better decipher the marketing hype surrounding you for each desired destination. Choose to do only those things that light you up.

I remember when my daughter and I stayed overnight in Munich, Germany. Before dinner, I took her to the Glockenspiel, a massive clock that is over one hundred years old and still operational. As we navigated through the cobbled streets toward Marienplatz Square, I excitedly recounted how the clock seemed to come alive as life-size figurines twirled and jousted to the chimes. I couldn't wait to show her! While waiting for the 5:00 pm bells to toll, crowds filled the square to witness the story of Munich's history told through the movement of the figures. Halfway through the reenactment, I looked over at my daughter to gauge her level of interest. She looked perplexed. "I don't get it," she said. "Why is everyone oohing and aahing?" And there you have it. One person's excitement is another person's snoozefest.

Theoretically, your travel bucket includes all the places you want to visit before you die (kick the bucket). The beauty of traveling solo and planning your perfect bucket list is that you only need to please yourself. There's power inside that bucket ready to transfer to you, solo sister. You are not promised unlimited time in life. Make your list or dust it off. Then, make that list come alive and dream on!

The Juice

Outbound for Bangkok

As I sit here waiting to board my flight to Thailand, I'm still in disbelief that after more than 20 hours of flight time from Denver to Singapore, I am finally on my way to tour Southeast Asia!

In truth, it's taken me about 40 years to get here. What was an outrageous dream in high school is about to become a reality! And I owe it all to the solo sisters around the globe who have shown me that anything is possible and that I can travel solo, too!

ENRICH YOUR EXPERIENCE

However you choose to travel, whether as a solo designing your own itinerary or as a solo on a group tour, it's worthwhile to make your trip more meaningful and memorable by enriching your planned experience.

The Meaningful Destination

You can expand your knowledge of an area by searching within a 200-mile radius to see if there is something special, you'd be sad to miss (and most likely to miss) if you stayed in your originating town. When I travel, I often look for nearby UNESCO sites because I enjoy learning about an area's significant historical or cultural perspective. For instance, I discovered a footpath from the coastal town of Perissa up to Ancient Thera, where I walked among the archeological ruins of a city dating back to the ninth century BC. This excursion made my time in Santorini so much more memorable because I was able to grasp how it felt to live back in the days of the ancient Greeks.

If you are particularly eco-minded, consider alternative travel destinations that offer a similar experience to highly touristed sites where you can still enjoy and protect the environment. Just read a story about the current conditions on Mount Everest, the cruel bullfights in Spain, or mistreated elephants in Thailand and India, and you will understand how carefully you should consider where you put your tourism dollars. Some attractions are more respectful of animal rights. Some less popular trails are just as beautiful as the more trafficked trails and don't cause damage to the environment. You decide based on what you value most.

The Perfect Souvenirs

While you can always find inexpensive trinkets and fun souvenirs in tourist kiosks to remind you of your travel destination, one of the most economical and beautiful ideas to capture and extend the memory of your trip is to take lots of photos, create a collage, or frame and display one stand-out photo. This is the best idea for someone with limited luggage space for souvenirs. I appreciate practical souvenirs representative of somewhere or something I experienced while traveling: tea towels from London, Connemara marble jewelry from Ireland, food gifts like olives from Greece or coconut candies from Hawaii, and scarves from Thailand. I also like to support local artists and buy ceramics or paintings to decorate my home. If you want to invest more, look up what the local artisans are crafting and search for reputable stores or galleries from which to purchase. In Greece, you'll find gorgeous bowls and furniture made of olive wood. In Japan, you will see precise examples of the ancient silk-screening technique of Katazome. In Bhutan, you will witness how they hand press large sheets of paper adorned with leaves and flowers. In India, specifically in Agra, you'll be mesmerized by marble pieces embedded with semi-precious stones just like those used in the construction of the Taj Mahal.

Displaying souvenirs like magnets and holiday ornaments, personal photos, or more elaborate artwork around your home is sure to prompt a smile and can lead to a fun conversation when someone visits. Remember what you buy, you must bring home. It helps to bring a packable tote bag to house your goodies for the flight back home.

The In-depth Education

Gain a deeper understanding of your destination by reading a book set in the exact location or written by an author who lived there. In northern Italy, I read a murder mystery set in the Tyrolean Alps. The author referred to several geographical and historical aspects of my visited area, and I instantly felt more connected with the mountains. Another option is to pick up literature about the area's history and notable figures. Before I went to Vietnam to visit the War Remnant Museum in Ho Chi Minh City, I read The Women, a book about female nurses who served in Vietnam during the war. I also wanted to understand the American perspective of war through film, so I viewed the 2002 film We Were Soldiers (sometimes with my hands covering my eyes) and listened to a memoir by a Marine veteran.

The Total Immersion

As you visit, the best way to make a place stick in your mind is to call on your five senses (smell, taste, touch, sight, and sound). Chew your food slowly and note the intricate spices used and which drinks are served with dessert.

Smell the fresh breezes in a nature preserve or appreciate the salty ocean aromas wafting from the local fish market. Glide your hand slowly over the silk tapestries and hanging scarves. Stare without blinking at the deep green towering trees or the kaleidoscope of blazing city lights. Close your eyes and listen to the random sounds of traffic at rush hour or the birds chirping before anyone else has risen. Of all the souvenirs you could choose, these will be the finest things you take away from your trip. Break out your journal and capture these moments so you can remember, over and over again, the beauty of this new and now familiar place.

The Juice

Skinny-dipping in the Sea of Cortez

The others had buttoned up their tents. I had been waiting for this moment all day.

Now was the perfect time to do that thing I had promised myself I would do.

It was so dark that the cloudy mix of the Milky Way galaxy shone through and cast a mysterious glow on the sunless sea.

Infused with pinprick burning lights, the ink-black sky capped off what I now can claim as one of the most memorable nights of my life.

I stripped down, except for my water shoes to offer my virgin soles some protection from the unavoidable mosaic of round rocks on my way into

I dove in.

Stroke. Swirl. Propel forward.

There was almost no need to breathe.

The light show of bioluminescence had begun.

A field of stars above me.

A field of aquatic sparkles in front of me, beside me, and under me.

At that moment, as never before, I was wrapped up in the snow globe of the Universe.

LESSONS FROM THE WORLD

If you ask someone about their latest trip, they will most likely enthusiastically share the highlight reel about what they did, who they did it with, and if they enjoyed the food. And, if anything went wrong, you'll hear about that, too. They'll scroll through their phones, looking for the perfect picture that captures it all. You might get lucky and hear a funny story if your conversation lingers.

Beyond the highlight reel lurks the potential for the real juice associated with travel. Observing how others live while being removed from your familiar environment can bring you new realizations about your life and what you can contribute to the world. Regardless of your age, you will begin to reflect on the person you are and, more importantly, develop a yearning to become the person you want to become. You undoubtedly will have your mind expanded and your faith in Humankind restored, especially if you travel abroad. Edith Wharton said, "One of the great things about travel is you find out how many good, kind people there are." With all these positive examples coming into your path, it's almost impossible not to want to try to be and do better.

And the solo travel thing? I believe it can increase your growth potential tenfold. When you are by yourself, you will be more spontaneous and make time to engage with the locals, and you won't be distracted taking a poll to determine where to go or what you will do next. Your senses will be alert and receptive to every kind of stimuli.

Case in point: I was solo hiking down a mountain road dotted with rows of oleander shrubs. Feeling glorious in the warm sun, I spread my arms wide (like Maria in The Sound of Music when she twirls on the top of the mountain). I gently slid my fingers along the leathery leaves as I floated by. And then I stopped in my tracks. Something didn't feel like a leaf. It was softer, squishier. I reversed my path and searched for a few minutes until I found the culprit nestled on a branch: a light green oleander hawk-moth caterpillar with two shiny blue eyes. He fascinated me because I had never seen a bug that looked just like an alien out of a comic book. I spent several minutes marveling at the various sections of his body and the patterned dots on his back. My discovery wasn't earth-shattering but added an enriching surprise to my hike. I would have been distracted and rushed if I had walked with someone else. I'm sure I wouldn't have been singing "The Hills Are Alive" in my mind or extending my arms out in the first place.

When I think back to the places I have had the privilege of visiting, it becomes evident that this world has shaped me far more than my parents have. No slight to Mom and Dad intended. You tend to accept and integrate more life lessons when you aren't resisting them from sheer rebellion! Some of these lessons have been heartbreaking, and some have been heartwarming.

In Bhutan, I witnessed examples of unshakable faith; in Iceland, I saw the pride of inherited tradition; in Patagonia, I was reminded that isolation or inclusion is always a choice. On my latest trip to Greece, I met a taxi driver who had given up his white-collar job in Athens. He moved back to Crete to support the family business, which had been struggling to recover since the pandemic. They had lost an entire fleet of cars and drivers, and the staff of over twenty-five was now just three. He said he missed the city terribly but was proud that he could serve his family. Then he put his hand over his heart and gave it a little thump. There was a visible dry gulp in his throat.

When I returned home from Greece, I started asking myself: How can I, with my whole heart, be in service to those I love the most? Perhaps I would have come to that question on my own. Here is what I do know: connecting with others through my solo travels teaches and reteaches me about the most important things in life.

What is your reason for traveling? Do you want to find love or forget it? Do you want more adventure or relaxation? Do you want to learn something new or be entertained? Do you want to make new friends or deepen your current relationships? Whatever the reason, solo sister, know you will get far more than you bargained for.

The Juice

Walking the Beaches of Puerto Natales, Chile

When is there time to quiet a shambolic mind?

Deeply.

Uninhibited.

Uninterrupted.

You can't get to this place without going it alone.

Dismiss casual conversations for now. You can always chat about the weather or where someone had dinner last night.

You will find yourself in this space you create for yourself, even if you weren't looking.

ABOUT THE AUTHOR

KIM DALZELL

An established author and professional speaker in the nutrition field, this is Kim's first book on travel, gleaned from her journeys to 25 countries.

Recently retired, Kim travels the globe searching for meaningful experiences while overcoming personal limiting beliefs. Her communication style is authentic and unfiltered. She desires to share the world's beauty while inspiring and motivating others to see the beauty in themselves.

Kim lives with her husband in Colorado, which is the perfect place for an avid hiker!

FROM THE AUTHOR

Dear Solo Sister,

Thank you for reading my contribution to your wanderlust, and I hope you have an incredible time traveling the world and filling your spirit with the juice of life.

If you've ever fantasized about living out one of your abandoned dreams from your youth, "Confessions of a Sticky Rice Girl" will make you laugh, cry, and reignite your adventurous soul.

Immerse yourself in the heartwarming and heartbreaking stories of solo travelers from different countries who unite to take on the physical rigors and emotional challenges of a one-month journey through five Southeast Asian countries armed with nothing but a backpack, a curious mind, and the spirit of youth.

I'd love to hear from you. Please connect with me on Facebook: DrKimDalzell

With love and admiration,

Kim

PS - If you have enjoyed my books, please help others find them by leaving a review on Amazon.

Printed in Great Britain
by Amazon

61477201R00117

Printed in the USA
CPSIA information can be obtained
at www.ICGtesting.com
LVHW021725021024
792743LV00003B/425

9 781648 300042